The Oil Crisis and Economic Adjustments

The Oil Crisis and Economic Adjustments

Case Studies of Six Developing Countries

Andrew MacKillop

edited by
Salah Al-Shaikhly

St. Martin's Press, New York

St. Martin's Press, Inc., 175 Fifth Avenue, New York, NY 10010
Printed in Great Britain
First published in the United States of America in 1983

Library of Congress Cataloging in Publication Data
MacKillop, Andrew.
The oil crisis and economic adjustments.
Includes index.
1. Energy policy – Developing countries. 2. Power resources – Developing countries. 3. Developing countries – Economic policy. 4. Economic history – 1971– 5. International economic relations. I. Shaikhly, Salah al-din, 1939– . II. Title.
HD9502.D442M32 1984 338.9'009172'4 83–40158

ISBN 0–312–58302–8

CONTENTS

PREFACE AND ACKNOWLEDGEMENTS

As the impact of the energy crisis began to be felt by developing and developed countries alike, international organisations and Western academic institutions began to promote what became popularly known as'conventional hypothesis' on the theory of adjustment. The Centre commissioned Andrew MacKillop to review the publications and statements of these institutions and to make a comparison between the forecasts of these institutions and what actually happened in developing countries. He produced the first draft which I then took upon myself to review and edit — aligning the various findings that he had presented

Mrs Veena Jha-Singh had the task of working together with the publishers' readers, making numerous corrections and adjustments and answering the queries raised by the publishers. I am grateful for her contributions and other efforts which she has put into this work. I am also grateful to Mrs Heather Bliss and Mrs Elizabeth Moore for reading the typescript of the book and pointing out relevant shortcomings in the flow of the subsequent drafts. I must also thank Miss Meg Peacock and Mrs Joan Peacock for originally typing and retyping the manuscript, without whose efforts this valuable work would have been much delayed.

Dr Salah Al-Shaikhly,
Executive Director,
Centre for Research on the New International Economic Order,
Oxford, England.
August 1983

PREFACE AND ACKNOWLEDGMENTS

INTRODUCTION

1. This study surveys the process of international economic and social change. Most of these economic changes have been described as 'economic adjustment'. This term is the very core of this study and in it the term, its corollaries, implications, and varied interpretations have been carefully analysed.

2. The processes described as 'economic adjustment' cover a wide spectrum. They are not in any way confined to the energy sector alone. The generality of their application is further extended by time, and by geographical dimensions. Nevertheless, both developed and developing North and South countries are adjusting their economies to changing factor prices, economic pressures, and new policies.

3. In the current era, however, economic adjustment has reached an intensity and a political importance hitherto unknown. The data sources on economic changes are not uniform. Therefore, a wide range of errors may be present in data on the same subject from different sources. Many examples can be cited, such as that of national debt. This is often presented (if presented at all) using complex definitions many months out of date and susceptible to many interpretations.

4. International economic adjustment is currently taking place in an environment which can be described, at best, as critical. As the current global recession intensifies, it becomes increasingly difficult to collect and interpret data. Energy is particularly easy to 'identify' as perhaps the single most significant factor among those causing economic stagnation, budgetary problems, national indebtedness, and so on. This is because 'energy', and particularly oil, is a single unitary factor of production, virtually ignored as a major economic factor until the mid-1970s.

5. It is, therefore, not surprising that there now exist quite well-

defined hypotheses which attribute the economic problems of the South (seen notably in the deficit developing countries) to the energy sector. A summary of such hyotheses provides this study with what can be termed the 'conventional hypothesis'. It is this conventional hypothesis, as advanced by agencies and institutions in both the North and the South (but particularly by the World Bank (IBRD) and certain UN agencies), that is analysed in detail throughout this study.

6. Briefly, the 'conventional hypothesis' states that the supply cost and financing of energy imports present a serious problem for most less developed countries (LDCs), especially the deficit LDCs. This hypothesis has many significant implications for the national investment programmes of developing countries, particuarly with regard to investment in sometimes costly 'alternative energy' schemes, now heavily advocated by the IBRD.

7. Because of their importance, certain of the study's conclusions (summarised in Chapter 8) can be referred to at this introductory stage. Of these, probably the most important is that which underlines the very serious and unwelcome interaction of two major economic changes currently operating at world level. On the one hand, economic adjustment in the North is almost exclusively concerned with protectionism and capital intensification of industry. On the other, the monetarist policy operated by several major industrial nations has increased the interest rates to historically high levels, while cutting commodity prices. At the same time, world trade has stagnated. Capital intensification of the North's industries can be a successful adjustment measure, provided that the market is expanding and that the relationship between interest rates and industrial growth is direct and certain.

Thus, at a time when both the industries of the North and the developing countries of the South are re-equipping, it is apparent that markets are stagnant or shrinking, interest rates are at record highs, and receipts by the south for primary product exports are deteriorating. This conjunction is a recipe for the bankruptcy of industries in the North, and of nations in the South.

8. It is possible that this briefly evoked conclusion may appear too sombre. It should, however, be noted that the world economy now shows clear signs of further deterioration. The fact that in 1981 just

nine large developing countries together accounted for more than 70 per cent of the total oil imports of all developing countries (7.3 million barrels per day) shows that this one factor — oil energy imports — cannot be the sole cause of the current economic deterioration. However, this study does show that energy and energy-linked policy changes have had an impact on the economic trends of many countries of the North and of the LDC group.

9. There was no intention of making the chosen sample for this study large enough to be statistically significant, and the choice of six sample countries for detailed study was made at random. Two developing countries were chosen from Asia, two from Africa, and two from the Latin American region to represent each of these region's poorer nations. As it turned out, the economic indicators of these countries were not significantly different from the regional averages for each group. The country studies, therefore, can be regarded more as individual case studies than as statistical samples. The intention of this study was to show that the increase in oil prices was not the sole reason for the economic malaise of the developing countries. The World Bank's and the IMF's own figures and analyses are used to show that there are clearly alternative ways of economic adjustment apart from the deflationary approach that these two international institutions have been preaching, and which they have attempted to enforce on developing countries.

1 ADJUSTMENT — THE 'CONVENTIONAL HYPOTHESIS'

1.1 Introduction

This study is primarily concerned with the social and economic changes which have come to be called 'adjustment'. The focus is on energy-linked, energy-constrained, and energy-determined aspects of adjustment. While adjustment concerns global economic change, this study is confined to developing countries, and within these a small sample of six have been chosen for special scrutiny.

1.1.1 Economic growth

The role of economic growth is of critical importance in assessing the economic (and other) changes which are broadly categorised as adjustment. Such changes can occur at the global, regional, national, or sectoral level. Conventional definitions of growth, such as those adopted by the World Bank (IBRD), are used in the study except where explicitly stated otherwise. The World Bank's and other such analyses are referred to as the 'conventional hypothesis' and this is contrasted with the hypothesis of this study, which is developed in Chapter 3.

1.1.2 World economic growth trends

The period between 1960 and 1973 was marked by high levels of economic growth all over the world. By comparison with the other period of major structural economic change (often referred to as the Industrial Revolution) in Europe, North America, and Japan,[1] when annual growth rates of 1.5 to 2.5 per cent were typical, the 1960–73 period showed far higher growth rates. During the period 1974–8, but especially after 1979, there was a marked decline in growth rates and in certain cases there was actually a net reduction in Gross National Product (GNP).

1.1.3 'Oil crisis' and adjustment

It is not coincidental that during the period (1960–73) of very high economic growth rates real oil prices and real non-oil commodity prices were stagnant or falling, while those of manufacturers and services were rising world-wide. From late 1973 until mid-1974, oil prices were increased through unilateral action by the major producers within the Organisation of Petroleum Exporting Countries (OPEC). This change was popularly termed by the Western media the 'first oil crisis' or the 'first oil shock', and was followed by spectacular increases in certain commodity prices, notably of sugar, coffee, gold, and copper.

During 1979 there were again large increases in posted oil prices. The popular media called it 'the second oil crisis'. However, the consequent economic and financial changes were different from those that followed the first oil price rise in 1973. Certain parallels and similarities, however, can and will be drawn throughout this study between the first and second sequence of 'oil-crisis', 'initial response', and 'adjustment'. These terms will be frequently used to condense the portrayal of the major changes that were taking place at many levels of the world economy during the period 1973–80. It should be clearly noted that causality, at this stage, is in no way attributed to this sequence.

1.1.4 The post-1979 period

From late 1978 to mid-1979 onwards, it is striking how rapidly and deeply the world economy has drifted into crisis and how it has been deliberately and systematically driven into deep recession. In some countries the economy was still showing rather high inflationary tendencies: after 1978, inflation rates were climbing in most industrial countries (the OECD countries and the United States) and in the majority of less developed countries (LDCs), but these were accompanied by a fast growth in interest rates, a development often described as the beginning of 'the interest rate war'. In 1980 these trends intensified, leading to the highest real interest rates since 1945 and the lowest commodity prices for decades. Since then, economic growth rates have plummeted, declining to around 5 per cent in some developing countries, while the level of world investment and trade has stagnated and, in certain sectors and countries, has actually decreased. In addition, unemployment rates in all countries have reached historic highs.[2] In many LDCs, particularly those with under $US400 per capita income, low rates of growth, high interest rates, and inflation have exacerbated their problems, especially the problem of rural poverty.

The seriousness of the evolving world economic situation has, of course, been particularly marked in the LDCs. However, despite the existence of a global economic recession, the 'conventional hyothesis' continues to explain the economic and development problems of LDCs in terms of the rise in oil prices. While the set of policy analyses which constitutes the 'conventional hypothesis' has been publicised by major development and financial institutions from 1978 onwards, it is only recently that it has come to be termed 'adjustment'. It should therefore be noted that this term is commonly used to describe and prescribe changes in the economies of the OECD countries, and thus the 'conventional hypothesis' largely provides an analysis of adjustment in these countries. However, because of their importance to this study, an analysis is provided of the LDC adjustment policies and programmes.

1.2 Data sources and problems

It is of critical importance to be aware of the unreliability of the data base upon which any analysis of large-scale, recent economic events (in both the North and the South) must be founded. There are many reasons for this, some of which are briefly identified and described in the following pages. Essentially, the data sources, and more particularly the mathematical hypotheses, that are from time to time presented in this study, have short time spans and, for the oil-producing developing countries, often draw upon data of unknown reliability. This makes for a continuing need for caution in the analysis of such data, even when they offer an apparently plausible explanation for events.

1.2.1. Definition of terms

A useful departure point for illustrating the problems of data assembly and analysis is that of the financial and economic sector. In analysis of this sector the actual level of current account deficits can vary by several per cent according to the definition of balance of payments utilised by each particular data source. A standard definition of the balance of payments is:

> [These are] traditionally defined as the record of a country's international transactions with the rest of the world (or in other words, transactions of its residents with non-residents), together with a very few transactions, such as the monetisation of gold, that do not fall under the main definition. The concept of the

> balance of payments may sometimes be broadened [to include other factors].[3]

On this basis, the current account is a restricted entity which is limited to transactions in goods, net financial services, etc., but which on occasions may also include official aid flow, which for many of the LDCs in the sample is sizeable in terms of GNP.

For the purposes of this study, except where explicitly stated, the balance of payments and the current account are taken to be closely and functionally related. Where possible, the two are separated. Similarly, GNP and Gross Domestic Product (GDP) (which, particularly for the lower-income developing countries, show quite large differences) are always clearly identified in this study.

However, the difference between GNP and GDP is sometimes treated as rather insignificant by the IBRD itself. The IBRD *World Development Report* of 1980 states that the current account deficits of LDCs '. . . rose sharply from 2.3% of their GNP in 1970 to 5.1% in 1975 and from 2.3% in 1978 to 3.9% in 1981'.[4] However, the 1981 report, under the section entitled 'A ten year perspective',[5] states that the current account deficit of LDCs in 1975 was 5.1 per cent of their GDP and that it reached 4.4 per cent of their GDP in 1980. Such variations can easily be attributed to a change in the accounting base(s) used from year to year; a change in currency equivalents and the consequent corrections; and/or data variations for a specific year compared with the time of data collection and analysis.

However, it is important to be aware that the IBRD makes the obvious error, on certain occasions, of equating GDP with GNP. Furthermore, a close comparison of the country data for 1970–7 in the IBRD *World Tables* of 1980[6] with the equivalent data in various editions of the IBRD *World Development Report* reveals significant differences. And when IBRD data on specific topics (such as the current account deficit in year A for country B) are compared with the data from other institutions, such as the Bank for International Settlements, the General Agreement on Tariffs and Trade, the Organisation for Economic Co-operation and Development, or the European Communities Commission, and so on, the differences between them is sizeable, easily reaching 25 to 33 per cent.

In addition, many of the information sources used in the IBRD *World Development Report* present apparently concrete equations (for example, for the projection of commercial energy demand) which, on closer examination, are found to be rather unreliable, due notably to the use of short time-series variables showing very high collinearity, and of data based on only a few, small, sample countries and which apply only to restricted sectors of energy demand, for example just electricity, or just industrial demand. As a result, in this study great caution has been exercised in making projections and analyses based on models which are not generally applicable or reliable.

Many examples of this problem could be cited. One brief example can be seen in the recent reports of the United Nations Economic and Social Commission for Asia and the Pacific (UNESCAP),[7] which considers commercial energy policy and its financial implications. The technical appendix of this report shows the regression equations used for predicting commercial energy demand per capita, in various years, based on four determinant variables. The projections made with these equations are claimed to be 'everywhere significant at the 5% level'. The equations have the general form:

$$\log CE = k + k_1 (1n\ GNP) + k_2 (1n\ URB) + k_3 (1n\ INDOP) - k_4 (1n\ TAX),$$

where:

CE = commercial energy demand per capita;
GNP = Gross National Product per capita;
URB = percentage urbanisation;
INDOP = percentage of industrial output in GDP;
TAX = percentage of indirect taxes in consumption; and
$k_1, k_2 \ldots k_4$ are constants, varying with time of projection (1972–8) and with correction for heteroskedasticity (a measure of variation within the total sample population used).

1.2.2 Numerical relationships

Differences in definitions from source to source and date to date can lead to significant problems of interpretation. These problems are far more severe with apparently precise, numerical relationships, particularly when mathematical equations identifying certain trends and relationships are utilised.

At the most basic level, numerical expressions of precise economic criteria for specified periods of time can vary quite significantly from source to source. A simple example can be seen in the estimates, from various sources, of GDP growth rates over recent periods for all developing countries and low-income developing countries. A summary of these estimates is shown in Table 1.1. The most extreme variation in this selection of GDP growth estimates is between the IBRD's and the Commonwealth Secretariat's figures for low-income developing countries in the period 1960–70, a variation of about 33 per cent. Other estimates, for the sample countries alone, also show quite large variations. Since the GDP growth of developing countries from 1960–70 was about $US650 billion (measured in 1979 dollars), rather small percentage variations have rather large quantitative impacts, at least equal, for example, to the oil account of LDCs outside the small group of major oil-importing developing countries.

The variation of the k constants over the period (for example k

Table 1.1 Real annual GDP growth rates, estimates from different sources for all developing countries and poorer developing countries for a specified period

	Percentage annual GDP growth rate		
Period	*All developing countries*	*Low-income developing countries*	*Source*
1960–73	6.1	3.3	*World Economic Outlook,* June 1981
1973–5	4.1	3.1	
1960–70	5.9	4.2	IBRD, *World Development Report,* New York, Oxford University Press, 1981
1970–80	5.1	3.0	
1960–70	5.3	3.1	Commonwealth Institute, *The World Economic Crisis,* Economic Paper 13, London, Commonwealth Secretariat, September 1980
1970–7	5.8	3.2	
1961–73	6.0	—	A. Pepic, *8th Roundtable Conference on Energy and Economic Development,* Zagreb, Institute for Developing Countries, 1980
1974–9	5.2	—	
1965–74	6.2	4.0	C. Baron, Discussion Paper 53, Development Planning Centre, Erasmus University, The Netherlands, 1980.
1974–7	4.9	4.5	

varying from 0.65 to 0.89 and k_3 varying from 0.56 to 1.00) indicates the fluidity of the 'fixed' variables in determining commercial energy use per capita. From such equations it should be easy to develop numerically based quantitative relationships between the GNP growth rate and the commercial energy demand growth rate, namely, the national income elasticity of energy demand (NIEE). However, the predictive capability of the above regression equation, like many others, is rather poor. If the stated relationship for 1978 is used, but (perhaps significantly) a negative sign is inserted before the first *k* constant (which the UNESCAP report does *not* do),[8] the equation is as follows:

$$\log CE = -0.89 + 0.71\ (1n\ GNP) + 0.46\ (1n\ URB) + 0.56\ (1n\ INDOP) - 0.37\ (1n\ TAX)$$

The resulting projections are as shown in Table 1.2. Although the UNESCAP report relates only to its member countries, and thus excludes Jamaica, the apparent generality of the regression equation indicates that it should be able to generate reasonable energy demand projections for this country also. However, as has been demonstrated, the resulting predictions are very poor.

This example also serves to underline the points made earlier relating to the use of apparently hard and concrete data and data relations in this subject area. A recent price elasticity study of car fuel demand in European Community (EC) countries[9] during 1956–76 (the period covering the first oil crisis) highlights this problem: '. . . after the crisis year 1973 here has been a complete break-

Table 1.2 Actual commercial energy demand per capita compared with the regression equation of predicted demand for Bangladesh and Jamaica, 1978.

	*Commercial energy demand per capita 1978 (kgce)**		
Country	*Actual*	*Predicted*	*Variation*
Bangladesh	41	106	158 per cent overestimate
Jamaica	1,823	2,288	26 per cent overestimate

*kgce — kilograms coal equivalent.

Source: All data on GNP, URB, etc. are taken from the IBRD *World Development Report* of 1980, which presents country data for 1978.

down underlying [long-run elasticity models] to the extent that the elasticities estimated in the past are no longer valid'. The Kouris study indicates that short-run elasticity relationships were much better at predicting car fuel demand in the EC countries during the oil crisis period because *secular*, or even structural, immobilities had been established during the period 1960–73, cars were regarded as basic consumer goods, and therefore the demand for petrol continued despite higher prices.

It will be argued later in this study that the majority of deficit developing countries, to the consternation of certain economists and observers in the North, have often responded to large oil price rises in the way typified by EC car owners, i.e. there was a stabilisation of demand rather than a collapse, with underlying structural and secular pressures soon reasserting the economic and social need for commercial energy, expressed as a re-establishment of oil and oil-based energy demand growth.

It is obvious from the foregoing discussion of data sources that this study's analysis of important events and relationships is unavoidably limited by highly disaggregated and unreliable data. (These events and relationships together account for rapidly changing regional and global economic factors — for example oil price rises.) As a result, this study cannot pretend the establishment of concrete and precise relationships. Rather, it seeks to identify and analyse (within the limits of the data) those hypotheses and viewpoints relating, in particular, to adjustment in certain developing countries.

1.3 Adjustment

It is basic to this study that a working definition of 'adjustment' be presented. At present, the definition of this term is still far from clear, since it is used in different economic, financial, or planning contexts to mean very different things. An IBRD report[10] defines the effect of oil-related economic changes as the massive enlargement of industrial and commercial activity, the growth of markets, and the beginning, perhaps, of the long-awaited Southward shift in the world's economic centre of gravity. The growth of primary producer cartels, of which OPEC is the *sine qua non*, has ensured a closer and more efficient linkage between factor supply and price. As was briefly witnessed in the recovery phase of 1975–9, non-oil primary product prices reacted quickly to buoyant demand as trade and investment surged ahead.

However, the question of oil price adjustment has come to receive a very special and precise set of policy prescriptions from the IBRD, the International Monetary Fund (IMF), certain UN agencies, such as the UN Industrial Development Organisation (UNIDO), and some special agencies, such as the OECD's International Energy Agency (IEA). The North's response to increased energy prices has also affected the deficit developing countries.

It is thus evident that a concrete set of policy responses and analyses has been developed by the various institutions. It is open to much criticism, as will become apparent in the course of this study. Recent issues of the IBRD's *World Development Report* have devoted more and more space to the topic of adjustment. For example, the IBRD *World Development Report* of 1981 devotes more than one-third (over 45 pages out of 120) of its discussion and analysis to oil price adjustment, almost exclusively in the developing countries. The bibliography of this report[11] lists some thirty-six IBRD staff working papers, and of these some nineteen are concerned with adjustment in developing countries. It is thus apparent that while various concrete expressions of adjustment can easily be made, a wider debate on its real implications is only just beginning.

For the purposes of this study, however, it is useful to utilise one of the IBRD's more recent definitions of adjustment, as outlined in the following extract from an IBRD report:

> As a consequence of the higher price for oil, all consuming nations have an incentive to economise in their use of energy; to develop alternative sources of petroleum; and where possible to substitute alternative forms of energy for petroleum.
>
> For the DDCs in particular there are two principal implications of the new level of petroleum prices:
>
> (i) in the short-term, given a very limited ability to conserve ... or substitute ... for petroleum, they must continue to borrow to maintain imports of oil ...
>
> (ii) in the longer-term most have the opportunity to develop alternative energy resources.[12]

The section in this report dealing with what is now called 'adjustment' goes on to remark that with higher oil price levels (1976 as against 1972) previously uneconomic oil resources become feasible for rentable development. The report also outlines the well-known problem of gaining the 'investor confidence' of multinational oil companies (whether independent or members of the 'Big-Seven') to encourage exploration and development outside the Middle East, North America, and Europe.

During 1979–81, however, the term 'adjustment' came to have a far more precise definition relating particularly to *economic* and *financial* strategies (i.e. short-term policies), and somewhat negating the role and importance of *energy* strategies and long-term policies. The IBRD's Report 466 of July 1981 thus has the significant title: *An Analysis of Adjustment in Oil-Importing Developing Countries.* This report develops a model for predicting the additional borrowing as a proportion of GDP and the interest elasticity of borrowing as a result of the 1979 oil crisis. The report notes in its preface:

> It is assumed that in the short run, immediately after the shock, the economy is rather inflexible, in the sense that substitution possibilities in production between energy and other inputs, and in consumption between traded and non-traded [goods], are low. As substitution possibilities increase, the required change in relative prices [with respect to the pre-shock situation] is less than in the first period. This becomes the rationale to borrow in the first period against subsequent periods, i.e. to bring foreign exchange towards the period when it is more scarce.[13]

It is quite easy to condense the definition of adjustment, whether in the context of developing or developed countries. This is because any rapid and sudden change of factor prices (in this case for oil-based energy) leads to two basic responses:

(i) changes in production patterns; and
(ii) changes in consumption patterns.

It is, of course, true that the manifestation of these changes can be relatively rapid or slow, ordered and planned, or spontaneous and accompanied by consequent financial problems or crises. As will be apparent in subsequent chapters, global economic changes, including energy-related 'adjustment', have been of great significance to the six sample developing countries. It will be shown that there is an irreducible minimum factor price adjustment which has significant impacts on consumption and production patterns.

1.4 The 'conventional hypothesis'

It has already been noted that during the period beween the first and second oil crises the IBRD and several other institutions revised their policy conceptions of 'adjustment'. A specialised and concrete set of analytical viewpoints on adjustment is now reaching maturity including, notably, a specialist vocabulary for explaining, rationalising, and developing policy in response to the external factor price changes (notably oil) and the changes in world economic activity (in which oil is a relatively small factor) which have affected the developing countries since 1973. However, an adjustment theory for developing countries that is primarily concerned with oil prices and imports inevitably means that these countries must accept a pattern of slower growth that presents great dangers for the poorer developing countries, in addition to posing very real threats to the security and stability of the world financial system.

Later in this study attention will be given to the meanings and implications of the adjustment which has affected not only the developing countries but also Europe and the United States. At this stage, adjustment can be seen as demanding of the developing countries a cut in growth, greater indebtedness, and perhaps a

Table 1.3 Major adjustment thesis as presented by IBRD, 1981

	Sectors		
Target countries	*Trade*	*Energy*	*Capital flows*
Developing countries	Expand exports, including diversion of agricultural commodities. Substitute imports only if economic.	Raise prices to encourage conservation. Exploration of indigenous sources.	Borrow to cover balance of payments deficits and to invest in structural adjustment.
OECD countries	Expand cheap imports. Avoid protection, make positive industrial adjustment.	Conserve. Switch to alternative sources. Support energy projects in developing countries.	Increase aid to poorer developing countries. Support petrodollars.

Source: IBRD, *World Development Report,* 1981, p. 118.

move towards self-sufficiency in the internal economy and an attempt to gain new export markets. As its major adjustment thesis the IBRD has chosen that with the most 'economic' and deflationary implications for developing countries, as can be seen from the brief summary of IBRD recommendations presented in Table 1.3. This prescription is, of course, unrealisable without the underpinning of a growing world market, industrial transfer from North to South, and better credit-related procedures.

In addition, recent theories on adjustment (typified by the IBRD) contain defects and errors at the conceptual level as well as in practice. Indeed, the overall view of this study is that it would have been more appropriate to formulate adjustment policies and targets for developing countries (as opposed to the OECD countries) in the period after the first oil crisis. Solutions of a kind, albeit unstable, had already emerged (as in the recovery period of 1974–9), and thus these spontaneous economic, financial, and energy policy trends towards adjustment are in this study given the attention they appear to merit.

Notes

1. See, for example, A. Thompson, *The Dynamics of the Industrial Revolution,* London, Arnold, 1973.
2. G. Renshaw, 'The view from the North', in Renshaw (ed), *Employment, Trade and North–South Co-operation,* — WEP Study, Geneva, ILO, 1981.
3. J. Alves, *The Balance of Payments — A Glossary of Terms,* Washington DC, Balance of Payments Division, IMF, 1979.
4. IBRD, *World Development Report,* New York, Oxford University Press, 1980, p. 3.
5. IBRD, *World Development Report,* 1981, p. 14.
6. IBRD, *World Tables* (2nd edn.), Baltimore, Johns Hopkins University Press, 1980.
7. UNESCAP, *Short-term Economic Policy Aspects of the Energy Situation in the ESCAP Region,* Bangkok, UNESCAP, 1981.
8. Without the negative sign before the first k constant the predicted figure for Bangladesh in 1978 would be 500 kgce (cf. Table 1.2).
9. G. Kouris, *The Price Sensitivity of Petrol Consumption and Policy Implications,* London, Economic Models Ltd., 1979.
10. IBRD, *World Development Report, 1981*
11. Ibid., pp. 125–7.
12. IBRD, *Minerals and Energy in Developing Countries,* Report 1588, Washington DC, IBRD, May 1977.
13. IBRD, *An Analysis of Adjustment in Oil-Importing Developing Countries,* Report 466, Washington DC, IBRD, July 1981.

2 WORLD ECONOMIC TRENDS 1970–1980

2.1 Introduction

The least developed countries started from such low levels of GNP that despite high rates of growth in the 1970s they faced massive problems during the post-oil crisis recessions. This holds true for certain oil-producing developing countries as well. Within these multiple, and in some ways complex, patterns of change and development, certain expressions of human need and legitimate aspiration became more widely known and better formulated. These included an increased awareness of mutual North–South interests and, indeed, the definition and significance of 'North' and 'South' — expressed, for example, in the Brandt Commission study. Yet the North still vastly dominates world trade, and its own adjustment is therefore critical to whatever may happen in developing countries. Within the developing countries, this six-country sample (in many ways not representative) has nevertheless shown all the characteristics and problems and, sometimes, successes of adjustment.

2.2 Trends and problems in the world economy, 1970–80

As already noted, the period 1960–73 was characterised by high annual economic growth rates for all regions of the world. This pattern seems to have changed after the first and second oil crises, but it is difficult to ascertain beyond any reasonable doubt that the rise in oil prices alone inflicted this change.

Table 2.1 shows that world and regional GDP growth rates fell precipitately during the period 1973–5. It is equally obvious that they recovered dramatically in the period 1975–9. Thus, it may be argued, some kind of recovery did take place. This is especially true for the developing countries as a group, which recorded about 93 per cent of its *belle epoque* (1960–73) average annual GDP growth in the period 1975–9, compared to only 82 per cent for the OECD countries. Bearing in mind that the United States and Western

Table 2.1 Growth of real GDP by region, 1960–1981 (annual average growth, per cent)

Region	*1960–73*	*1973–5*	*1974–9*	*(estimate) 1979–81*	*Approximate percentage of 1979 world activity*
World	5.5	1.5	4.4	2.1	100.0
Developing countries	6.1	4.1	5.7	4.3	19.50
US	4.1	—1.1	4.5	1.5	23.50
OECD	4.8	0.7	3.4	0.6	29.50
Japan	10.4	0.5	6.0	4.0	9.75
OECD (North)	5.0	0.1	4.1	1.4	64.50

Source: 'World economic outlook', *Financial Times*, London, 2 July 1981.

Europe have a combined GDP three times that of all developing countries, it is interesting to note that the United States showed a particularly strong recovery, while Europe did not. Structural, financial, and policy differences, relative to adjustment needs, can explain this, as will be seen in later chapters.

As specific conclusions for the six sample countries cannot easily be made from these trends, it is useful to look also at post-1979 changes in world trade, divided into two main groups — 'all goods' and 'manufactured goods'. The first group, which includes all the primary non-oil commodities, is the major export and hard-currency earner of all the sample countries. It is notable, therefore, that while trade in the first group continued to flow at high rates during the period 1973-5, since late 1979 it has decelerated far below the growth rate for manufactured goods. Table 2.2 shows that world trade managed to grow well above population growth (average world population growth in 1970–80 was about 2.1 per cent per annum), except in the post-1979 recession. This has had very important effects on all the sample developing countries which, like the majority of developing countries, have rather small, growing, open economies, dependent on large external markets. Thus the recent slowing of world trade, combined with other negative factors (interest rates, capital costs of infrastructure, oil prices, etc.), reinforce the prognosis of accelerating financial, economic, and development problems for developing countries, particularly the most 'exposed' middle-income developing countries.

Table 2.2 Average annual world trade growth, 1968–1980 (per cent)

Category	*1968–78 average*	*1979*	*1980*
All goods	6.5	5.75	1.5
Manufactured goods	7.5	5.25	4.5

Source: National Institute for Economic and Social Research, quoted in *Financial Times*, London, 27 January 1981.

2.2.1 Trends in manufacturing

The 1970s, and perhaps more so the 1980s, marked the arrival of certain middle-income developing countries as serious contenders in domains previously regarded by the North as restricted territory (i.e. both Northern OECD and Socialist bloc countries).

Table 2.3 Share of industrial imports to the United States (per cent) in the period 1970–1981

Exporter group	*1970*	*1979–80*	*1980–81*
Developing countries	under 10	20.5	24.5
OECD (Europe)	Over 35	27.0	26.4
Japan	Under 20	26.0	27.2

Source: P. Judet, *Les Nouveaux Pays industriels*, Paris, Ouvrières, 1982.

As shown in Table 2.3, the growth of the manufacturing sector in the developing countries can be portrayed by their expanding share in the industrial imports of the United States. This growth was almost exclusively concentrated in the middle-income developing countries, particularly Brazil, South Korea, Taiwan, Hong Kong, Singapore, Mexico, and (low-income) India. Specific sectors have, of course, shown considerably more growth than others, in particular such well-known targets for tariff and non-tariff protection as clothing, leather, footwear and travel goods, wood and cork goods, textiles, and certain non-metallic mineral manufactures. There are strong arguments for encouraging adjustment by increasing the output of these and other industries in developing countries, as will be seen later. This component of industrial adjustment forms a significant part of West German and French economic policy, recently reinforced for the latter in the IXth National Plan.

The growth of certain newly industrialised developing countries within the group of middle-income developing countries has been very high in the past decade. But this must not obscure two very important factors, which are that:

(i) the industrial and manufacturing growth of developing countries has been concentrated in a few newly industrialised developing countries, and has taken place from low base levels; and
(ii) other developing countries have not shared in this growth, which is in any case threatened by the North's major protective and policy measures, which still dominate most industry.

These factors have had enormous implications for development efforts in the six sample countries (for example South Korea and Brazil), which have not had the opportunity to profit from very low interest rates and low energy prices in periods of flourishing world trade growth.

The continuing overall dominance of the North in the industrial exports sector can be seen from the data given in Table 2.4, which serves to underline the point that very high annual growth rates should not be allowed to obscure the relatively low base of activity. The small base also implies that industrial development, and the consequent growth, may be unstable and brief. This is especially marked in the smaller developing countries in the sample. In turn,

Table 2.4 Trade patterns in OECD/OPEC developing countries, 1978–1979 (1978 $US)

Country group	*Total imports*	*Total exports*	*Of which exports to OECD countries*	*Percentage of total exports to OECD countries*
OECD	216	200	—	—
OPEC	90	136	107	78.7
Developing countries	150	120	109	90.8
Manufacturing trade:				
OECD	41	163	—	—
OPEC	73	1.5	1.1	67
Developing countries	96.5	46	40	86.9

Source: G. Renshaw, 'The view from the North', in Renshaw (ed), *Employment, Trade and North–South Co-operation*, WEP Study, Geneva, ILO, 1981.

this helps to explain the variability and changes from year to year in the exports and industrial growth of the smaller, less developed countries.

Manufacturing growth for all developing countries has also been affected by the complex of negative trends affecting the world economy in general, notably of the 1973–5 and post-1975 recessions in the North, rising real interest rates, and structural imbalances in industrial economies. The growth rates of industrial output in developing countries during the period of this study, and agricultural output has fallen for all developing countries, as is shown in Table 2.5. The decline in annual growth rates for manfuacturing is serious enough, particularly as the expansion of industrial output and exports is the only secure method for easing the financial gap of middle-income developing countries. But the sharp drop, from an already low growth rate, of food and soft-commodity output is probably much more serious. This problem affects several of the sample countries, particularly Bangladesh, and most sub-Saharan African countries in general. There are, obviously, many reasons for this structural imbalance, but the pursuit by developing countries of industrialisation and urbanisation — supported, of course, by most international development institutions — is a major, unacknowledged, cause. Noting that the mismanagement of development has been a major factor in the complex of problems affecting developing countries, the director-general of the OPEC Fund recently remarked:

Table 2.5 Sectoral growth in developing countries, 1965–1979 (annual average growth, per cent)

	Agriculture			*Manufacturing*		
Sector Group	*1965-70*	*1970-7*	*1970-9*	*1969-70*	*1970-7*	*1970-9*
All developing countries	3.4	2.7	3.0	7.5	7.4	6.0
Middle-income developing countries	3.3	3.0	3.0	7.9	7.2	5.7
Poorer developing countries	3.0	3.0	2.0	3.3	5.2	4.2

Source: IBRD, *World Tables*, Baltimore, Johns Hopkins University Press, 1980; and IBRD, *World Development Report*, New York, Oxford University Press, 1981.

> ... a good part of the dilemma which developing countries are facing at present may be of their own making. There is no denying that external factors have turned the situation from bad to worse ... But this may present only half of the truth. For it is also true that most developing countries are doing little or nothing to check the menacing growth rates of their population, or to rationalise their patterns of consumption. Meanwhile efforts abound for increasing their military expenditure and multiplying their prestige projects.[1]

Price tags can quite easily be attached to the agricultural development needs of developing countries: for example in 1980, figures of $US35–45 billion per year were frequently advanced for this purpose.[2] Over the last decade, agricultural development has been de-emphasised by most developing countries, and the concurrence of energy-linked adjustment pressures and a food-related development problem now weighs upon the overall formulation of planning and development.

2.2.2 Trends of developing countries' finance

It has become a commonplace, almost automatic response to equate developing countries' rising current account deficits with the oil crises. A brief quotation from the IBRD illustrates this: 'After the first oil price increase, the current account surplus of all oil exports rose from USD 4.1b in 1973 to 62.2b in 1974. The mirror image of this was reflected in the deficits of all oil importers, both industrial and developing, in almost equal shares.'[3]

Both oil crises have been described as 'sudden deflationary shocks' to the world economic system, but one can easily argue that the first oil crisis at least was *not* deflationary, and that in its relation to developing countries' deficits (see Table 2.6)[4] there was no simple, one-to-one change of deficits (by developing countries and OECD countries) for surpluses (by all oil exporters). From the figures shown in Table 2.6 it is possible to draw a number of tentative preliminary conclusions. Many of these conclusions have major implications for the central aim of this study, which is to review in special depth the economic adjustment processes in developing countries.

Firstly, the current account deficits of developing countries have unquestionably increased throughout the decade 1970–1980. That said, one must note that the 1975 deficit was very close to that of 1980, and that of 1978 was below that of 1974. Yet 1980 was the first full year after the second oil crisis, and by 1978 the rapidly rising trend of private bank loans at variable (real) interest rates was beginning to have a marked impact.

Secondly, notable differences are apparent between the current account deficit pattern of the oil-importing North, and that of the developing countries. The developing countries' pattern was one of continuous deficits, rising slowly and unevenly throughout the period, while the North's showed considerable quantitative (although not always in relation to GNP) deficits and surpluses. It might be argued that the OECD countries showed a rapid response to the oil crises, while the developing countries showed a rather more delayed, or 'smoothed', response; however, it must be stressed that there is almost no hard, statistically valid relationship between oil price increases and current account deficits, or increases in such deficits. As shown in Table 2.6, the deficit on fuels trade of developing countries (of which about 85 per cent was due to oil in 1973–4, and over 80 per cent in 1979) increased by $US6.8 billion from 1973–5, but the current account deficit of developing countries increased by $US37.2 billion in the same period. Similarly, the fuels trade deficit from 1978–9 increased by only $US6.2 billion, but the current account deficit increased by $US24.2 billion. Not only are the two figures in each period grossly different but the

Table 2.6 Major changes in the current account deficits of all developing and OECD countries in selected years, 1970–1980 ($US figures at 1978 prices)

Category	*1970*	*1973*	*1974*	*1975*	*1976*	*1977*	*1978*	*1979*	*1980*
Developing countries' current account deficit ($US billions)	18.5	11.6	26.7	49.8	29.1	27.4	25.5	49.7	58.0
Increase (+) or decrease (−) on year before (per cent)	—	−33.0	+130.0	+86.0	−69.0	−6.0	−7.0	+95.0	+17.0
OECD countries' current account deficit or surplus (+) ($US billions)	+13.0	+18.0	8.3	+11.7	3.3	9.0	+24.2	12.5	31.7
Developing countries' current account deficit as a percentage of GDP	1.9	2.4	—	5.1	—	—	2.3	—	3.9
Developing countries' trade deficit ($US billions)	—	14.7	17.8	29.8	42.9	—	54.6	—	69.3
Developing countries' deficit on fuels ($US billions)	—	3.2	9.7	10.0	—	—	15.0	21.2	36.0
Developing countries' deficit on manufactured goods ($US billions)	—	26.9	32.8	36.6	—	—	55.5	63.5	68.8
Developing countries' deficit on fuels as a percentage of trade deficit	—	21.7	45.1	33.5	—	—	35.0	39.0	52.0
Capital services ratio*	14.5	13.4	11.1	11.9	11.5	12.9	15.5	15.0	—

* The capital service ratio is defined as: 'Contractual service payments on long-term debt, plus remitted profits on direct foreign-owned investment as a proportion of exports (goods and financial services).'

Sources: IBRD, *World Tables,* 1980; IBRD, *World Development Report,* 1980, 1981; *Le Monde, Bilan économique et social 1981,* Paris, *Le Monde,* 1981; and OECD, *Economic Outlook,* Paris, OECD, various issues.

ratio of one to the other in 1978/79, as against that in 1973/75, is very different. Thus, between the oil crises, while the current accounts deficit rose, the fuels deficit remained fairly constant. This relationship can be summarised quite simply, as is shown in Table 2.7.

Table 2.7 Trade (fuel and other imports) as a proportion of the GDP of all developing countries, selected years 1970–1980 (per cent)*

Category as a percentage of GDP	*1970*	*1975*	*1978*	*1980*
Fuel imports	3.3	2.6	2.8	2.7
Non-fuel imports	21.8	21.0	19.9	20.2
Current account deficit	2.4	5.2	2.3	4.4

* Data are at constant 1978 prices.
Sources: IBRD, *World Development Report*, 1981; and OECD, *Economic Outlook*, various issues.

If anything, these figures (Table 2.7) allow us to argue for a rather remarkable *consistency* in the fuel/other imports relationship — with current account deficit increases requiring some additional or, indeed, alternative explanations. However, despite this, the IBRD has permitted itself (as may have other development institutions) to develop tight, numerically based equations relating to oil price increases and *reductions* in GDP growth for developing countries.

Table 2.8 GDP growth and oil price rise relations for poorer developing countries and middle-income oil-importing developing countries, 1980–1990

	Real rate of oil prices growth 1980 (per cent)		
	0	*3*	*5*
Poorer developing countries' annual average GDP growth (per cent)	4.3	4.1	4.0
Middle-income developing countries' annual average GDP growth (per cent)	6.1	5.7	5.2

Source: IBRD, *World Development Report*, 1981, Table 2.9.

These have been presented in the IBRD *World Development Report* of 1981, as shown in Table 2.8, and take the form of predicted rates of GDP growth throughout the 1980s, under varying real oil prices, for poorer and middle-income developing countries. It is easy from these figures to develop an elasticity function between oil price rises and reductions in GDP growth rate brought about either directly or indirectly by oil price rises. This is shown in Table 2.9.

Table 2.9 Elasticity of GDP growth in oil-importing developing countries with certain rates of oil price growth, 1980–1990

Reduction in GDP growth for each per cent real oil price rise	*Real oil price increases (per cent)*			Average *coefficient**
	0—3	*3—5*	*0—5*	
Poor oil-importing developing countries (per cent)	—0.1	—0.1	—0.1	—0.06
Middle-income oil-importing developing countries (per cent)	—0.4	—0.5	—0.9	—0.16

* The average coefficient is the elasticity coefficient averaged over the years 1980–90.

Source: Author, derived directly from IBRD data.

At this point in the study it is not necessary to argue the rationality (given certain highly specific economic data) of such predictive equations. What is important at this point is that such equations are *offered at all*. In very broad terms, it can be argued that the IBRD's analysis (as shown in Tables 2.8 and 2.9) carries a strong deflationary message in a period when the interest rate problem alone (aside from basic human needs) demands a steady and real increase in developing countries' GDP. Therefore it is to this sector — the direct financial problems and pressures on developing countries — and its relationship with the oil crises that attention is now directed.

In the developing countries' finance sector it is important to note at least three large changes which have occurred during the period of this study, namely:

(i) a large increase in borrowing by middle-income developing countries;
(ii) stagnation in the role of Official Development Assistance (loans and grants);
(iii) the emergence of private international banks as the largest supplier of loans to developing countries.

Thus the total amount of concessionary (low-interest or zero-interest loans, and grants) and non-concessionary finance flowing to all developing countries increased from around $US19 billion in 1975 to nearly $US100 billion in 1980, but of this the vast majority (over 90 per cent) was obtained by middle-income developing countries, mostly as non-concessionary finance. The roles of factors (ii) and (iii) can be appreciated from the data shown in Table 2.10, which relates financial flows to sources for the years 1970, 1975, and 1978.

Table 2.10 Total financial flows to developing countries, selected years 1970–1978 ($US billions at 1978 prices)

Type and sources	*1970*	*per cent*	*1975*	*per cent*	*1978*	*per cent*
Concessionary						
DAC countries, bilateral	5.7	29.7	9.8	18.4	13.1	16.4
Multilateral agencies	1.0	5.2	3.6	6.7	5.0	6.2
OPEC, bilateral and multilateral	0.4	2.1	5.2	9.8	4.0	5.0
Socialist bloc	1.0	5.2	1.4	2.6	1.3	1.6
Non-concesionary						
Direct investment	3.7	19.2	10.6	19.9	11.2	14.1
Private bank loans	3.0	15.6	12.0	22.5	22.5	15.7
Private and OECD export credits	2.8	14.6	5.6	10.5	13.0	16.3
Total financial flows to developing countries*	19.2	—	53.3	—	79.7	—
Per cent concessionary		42.2		37.5		29.4

* Excluding oil-importing developing countries and OPEC export earnings.

Source: Editorial, 'The gap in international resource transfers to the 3rd world', *Development Dialogue*, **1**, 1981.

The figures in Table 2.10 show that concessionary finance from Official Development Assistance (ODA) was nearly equal to private bank loans in 1970, but that by 1978 the banks were lending 70 per cent more finance to developing countries than that obtained from ODA. Since then the role of the private banks has further increased, as has that of bank-related financial sources, such as the other categories shown under 'non-concessionary finance' in Table 2.10. This pattern is self-maintaining and even self-intensifying, and will therefore continue for a considerable period unless there are massive ODA increases from the North, including the Socialist bloc, at least equal to those advanced in the Brandt Report.[5] One factor, for example, which perpetuates this pattern is the interest rate structure of the world financial system.

While International Development Association assistance (OECD-funded multilateral finance), OPEC Fund, ODA grants, and other non-market, concessionary finance is provided at either 2 to 3 per cent interest or less (for example grants), private bank loans are of course lent at much higher rates. Throughout the early 1970s, as noted by the IBRD in its 1981 *World Development Report*,[6] the reality of high inflation and fixed private bank loans at somewhere below the inflation rate was a kind of safeguard to developing country borrowers. The reality of negative real interest rates and growing trade receipts assured a safe margin for manoeuvre in setting development targets. But in the later 1970s variable interest rates (VIRs) became dominant in private bank loans to developing countries. Variable interest rates are set in relation to the Lombard rate[7] and always show a 'spread', or premium, above Lombard to reflect developing countries' loan status, country risk, and other factors used to set loan rates to developing countries.[8] Combined with the spread, from 1978–9 onwards, of harsh deflationary and anti-inflationary policy measures in the OECD countries of the North, VIRs have ensured a rapidly rising debt burden for developing countries, adding to a debt that was already substantial in the mid-1970s.

The effects of high real interest rates, plus commodity prices at twenty-year lows (in real terms), slackened trade growth, and the oil price crises, among other factors, have led to a financial crisis situation for developing countries. Although financial problems are dealt with elsewhere in this study, it is important to mention here the steady escalation of defaults on loans made by private banks to developing countries during the 1970s, an escalation which has recently accelerated dramatically. Table 2.11 shows that the amounts defaulted have risen radically, even if Poland and South

Table 2.11 Trend of developing countries' (plus Mexico and Indonesia) defaults on loans: dates and approximate amount defaulted ($US billions)

Country	*Date*	*Amount*
Indonesia		
Philippines	1970	0.5
Ghana		
Pakistan	1974	—
Argentina	1976	—
Peru	1978	5.1
Turkey		
Jamaica	1979	—
Sudan		
Zaïre	1980	—
Poland	1981	2.5+
Zaïre	1981	0.9
Mexico	1982	4.5+
South Africa	1982	1.1

Sources: Indonesia-Zaïre 1980 inclusive — IBRD, *World Development Report*, 1981; Poland-SouthAfrica inclusive — *Le Monde*, Paris and *Financial Times*, London, various dates.

Africa are excluded — and on actual GNP per capita terms it should be noted that South Africa is a high middle-income developing country, extremely dependent on commodity exports. If this pattern is not to be repeated, possibly bringing about the worst-yet world financial crash, it is vital that the developing countries recover as buoyant export markets for the OECD countries, able to pay back loans while achieving real economic growth. Never before has the choice for world political leaders been more stark, or more important.

2.2.3 Adjustment in the OECD countries

The preceding review of finance, trade, and other economic trends in the developing countries clearly indicates that industrial development and trade growth offer important, and perhaps the only, routes out of the deepening financial and development crisis of the South. It is therefore critical to comprehend the emergence and application of 'adjustment' in the North, since its market is growing more slowly than markets in the South for exports from the South[9] and will remain quantitatively dominant for at least the next decade, and probably longer, whatever growth rates are achieved by the South. As noted previously in this chapter (and as outlined in Tables 2.2 and 2.4) inter-South trade is very small in relation to North–South trade.

The basic possibilities for industrial and economic trade and investment policies in the OECD countries, relative to the South, can be summarised as shown in Table 2.12. This table outlines certain possible responses by the industrial North to the growth of industry in the South, but very often national, even in-country regional, political pressures have led to a rather rapid growth of tariff and non-tariff barriers against the faster growth of imports from the South in specific countries and sectors.[10] The calculation of what such barriers to market access may or may not do to the growth of activity, GDP, exports, and loan needs of developing countries has shown spectacular growth. A specialist literature, with its own vocabulary and data treatment, has grown to explain what rate of growth Southern exporters might achieve, were it not for barriers, under various scenarios of trend growth in exports, and so forth.[11]

Table 2.12 Major adjustment opportunities for industrial countries, relative to the growth of industrial activity in the South

Policy response	*Impacts*
Reindustrialise	Identify and support new, skill-intensive industries; renew/upgrade infrastructure.
Skill growth	Change from low-skill to high-skill industries and services.
Secular change	Reduce exposure to more-efficient competition from the South, perhaps leave certain industries entirely.
Outward processing and integration	Relocate lower-skill, labour-intensive industries in the South; admit and facilitate market entry of Southern producers in selected industries; integrate Southern producers in production and marketing systems.

Based on: ILO, *Employment, Trade and North–South Co-operation,* Geneva, ILO, 1981.

An analysis of the effect of trade and tariff barriers on exports from developing countries to the North is outside the scope of this study, more especially since this 'rising tide of protectionism' is a phenomenon of the later, rather than the early, 1970s, and concerns only small numbers of 'threatened jobs'. Current estimates put the possible job losses in OECD Europe, the United States, and Japan from the elimination of all non-tariff barriers, and a 50 per cent average tariff reduction on *industrial* exports from the South, at well below 0.1 per cent of the cited Northern countries' industrial labour force[12] over the next ten years. Much more important for several of the sample countries are tariff and non-tariff barriers on *agricultural* exports from the South.

As will be noted in the chapter dealing with country adjustment, tariff, non-tariff, and technological barriers to the continued access of agricultural commodity exports from many developing countries to the North have caused severe problems. Here it can be noted briefly that Jamaica's sugar industry has been gravely damaged, in just five years, by EEC support (including tariff measures) for European beet-sugar producers, and by the development in the United States of the manufacture of new, non-sugar maize-based sweeteners at prices much below those required by the South's cane-sugar industries. Similar arguments apply to trade and market conditions for: Sri Lanka (tea); Senegal (peanuts); Bangladesh (jute); Kenya (tea, and coffee to some extent); and also, in time and in varying proportions, to the mineral exports of Peru (copper); and Jamaica (aluminium). While barriers on industrial exports from the South may be a dramatic, symbolic expression of the South's struggle for a better share in world trade, the constant erosion of agricultural terms of trade, and its impact on development and dependence, cannot be ignored. This is not to argue that trade barriers to Northern markets for Southern industrial exports are not important. The growth of such exports has played a catalytic and basic role in the growth of the newly industrialised countries. But in view of protectionism in the North, which is becoming increasingly politicised,[13] and in view of increasing *inter-South* competition in industrial goods markets, can the newly industrialised countries' growth model of the 1950s to the 1970s be regarded as an appropriate and *unique* development model?

This question posed, it is highly significant to note that few developed, and virtually no newly industrialised countries, disagree on the positive role of the first adjustment policy response shown in Table 2.12, and most also resort to measures that conform with the second response (skill intensification). But this improvement of infrastructure, better training, and new industrial plant is costly, demands much capital investment and time, and requires a fortunate and supportive external environment, notably a growing market. The transfer from industries such as food, beverages, and tobacco (with a high ratio of less-qualified to skilled workers, and relatively low capital investment per worker) to industries such as chemicals, electrical machinery, and road vehicles often requires a tenfold increase in capital.[14]

Certain developed countries, and the newly industrialised countries, have been highly successful at effecting this transfer, or continuing it in the case of such nations as Japan, West Germany, and France. If the growth of high value-added exports (for example electrical consumer goods and specialist chemicals) is continuous and rapid, then oil price crises may only cause a short, if severe, downturn in the current account. A notable example of this among the newly industrialised countries is South Korea, and among developed countries Japan can be cited. South Korea's adjustment to higher oil prices is given special praise and attention in the IBRD *World Development Report* of 1981.[15] A report on South Korea, which also examines Korean adjustment to the second oil crisis,[16] makes the following point about South Korea's adjustment to the first oil crisis:

> In 1973 the commercial energy system was more than 60% based on imported oil . . . and this was supplying more than 90% of the fuel for electricity production. Korea had succeeded in gaining a good penetration of commercial markets in Saudi Arabia, Kuwait and Iraq (Korea's main oil suppliers) and maintained a strongly positive commercial balance with these countries.
>
> The first oil crisis broke this equilibrium without slowing for one moment the increase of oil consumption, as the country maintained its economic growth. Oil consumption doubled from 1973 to 1979. During this period the revenue effect (increased exports and GNP) always overcame the

price effect (more costly oil) and nothing could slow energy demand growth.

This 'adjustment' bears little relationship to that proposed by the IBRD for developing countries in general. Neither would it appear that the apparently definitive 'oil price/GDP growth' relationship (showing a decrease in growth of GDP relative to an increase in oil prices — see Tables 2.8 and 2.9), which is much stronger and more direct for middle-income developing countries than for poorer developing countries (higher coefficient), is supported by the South Korean evidence. South Korea showed a dynamic *increase* in growth of exports, and a very large increase in the share of GDP devoted to investment, following the first oil crisis. It can be argued that this outward-oriented, growth-seeking policy response was able to aid South Korean adjustment more rapidly than policies based on the supposedly inevitable requirements to accept slower growth.

Table 2.13 GDP and productivity growth, five major OECD countries, selected years 1974–1979 (annual average, per cent)

Country	*1974*	*1976*	*1977*	*1978*	*1979*	*1979/ 1976–8*
USA						
GDP	−1.1	4.1	5.9	4.0	2.75	0.59
Productivity	—	2.7	1.3	−0.2	0.0	0.10
Japan						
GDP	−1.0	6.3	5.3	5.5	5.5	0.96
Productivity	—	5.4	4.0	4.3	4.5	0.98
West Germany						
GDP	0.4	5.7	2.5	3.4	3.75	0.96
Productivity	—	6.6	2.7	3.1	3.25	0.83
France						
GDP	3.3	5.2	3.0	3.8	3.0	0.83
Productivity	—	5.1	2.4	3.1	2.75	0.82
UK						
GDP	0.5	2.1	1.0	2.4	0.5	0.33
Productivity	—	2.9	0.6	2.1	0.25	0.17

Source: G. Renshaw, *Employment Growth and Basic Needs, A One-World Problem* (2nd edn.), Geneva, ILO, 1978.

As shown in Table 2.13, five major industrial countries also showed a re-establishment of growth from 1976, after the first oil crisis, and it can be argued that Northern policy, after an initial hesitation of twelve to eighteen months, in some aspects followed the lead of the South Korean and other newly industrialised countries' adjustment. It is useful to note that most (four out of five) of these major industrial countries showed vèry low, or negative, growth rates in 1976–9. Apart from the United Kingdom and the United States, their rates of investment exceeded 20 per cent of GDP throughout this period.[17] Thus in 1979 their growth and productivity rates did not fall to the same extent as those of the United Kingdom and United States. Since 1979, however, both GDP growth and productivity growth have been low or negative in virtually all industrialised countries,[18] indicating that adjustment to the second oil crisis — if this is the prime factor — is taking somewhat longer to effect.

The effects of the first oil crisis on the economies of the oil-importing developed countries were in many ways similar to the response pattern of the developing countries. The *extent* and *continuity* of the energy import dependence of the major OECD countries can be gauged from the ratio of imported to total energy consumption of all kinds, which for West Germany, France, and Italy stood at 58, 64, and 82 per cent respectively in 1981,[19] after seven years of 'dependence-reduction' energy policies and large investments such as that of the EEC Commission energy budget, which in 1979 was 241 million ECU (about $US250 million).[20] Thus the first oil crisis led rapidly to a worsened current account, changing the 1973 surplus to a significant deficit. Within twelve to fifteen months the 'recycling of petrodollars' had achieved very significant increases in private (and state) bank liquidities.[21] In the inflationary conditions of 1973–5, for certain OECD Northern countries (as shown in Table 2.13), 'petrodollar deposits' became in reality negative interest loans, but high inflation led to serious *internal* economic difficulties for the OECD countries. This cheap capital influx radically improved lending capacities, while mitigating trends towards competitive devaluations, which have recently (1981–2) become marked.

In essence, economic and industrial policy for the major OECD countries during the first oil crisis adjustment period was torn between a deflationary response due to higher inflation, and an inflationary and expansionist response due to a rather rapid trend away from existing trade patterns with developing countries. These responses can be appreciated from the summarised data given in Table 2.14, which shows approximate directional trends in North–South trade up to 1973, and in 1976–8. The decreasing importance of developing countries as export markets for the North from 1955–73 was most evident in exports to the poorer developing countries, whose share decreased by a greater proportion than that for all developing countries.

Table 2.14 North–South trade by direction, 1955, 1973, and 1976–1978 (per cent)

	Proportion of all exports		
Direction of trade	*1955*	*1973*	*1976–8*
North to all developing countries	55	20	30+
North–North	34	76	65

Source: C. Stevens (ed), *The EEC and the Third World*, London, Hodder and Stoughton, 1981.

The first oil crisis, therefore, reversed this declining trend in the importance of the South as a market for the North, particularly for the Capital Surplus Oil Exporter countries and for the middle-income developing countries. This pattern was further reinforced by the vast increase in private bank loans and commercial credits, fuelled by petrodollars. The total dominance of just a few middle-income developing countries as beneficiaries of this recycling can be seen from statistics on Euromarket lending to developing countries. Of the total funds loaned in 1979, some 99.7 per cent went to Argentina, Brazil, South Korea, and Mexico.[22] Until recently, Brazil and Korea were regarded as model examples of oil price adjustment because of their aggressive growth-oriented export policies, which were able to benefit from the stimulated, growing world market conditions of 1976–9.

However, trade trends reinforcing North–North economic links ensured much closer cyclicality and integration of economic impacts and changes within the North. Thus the rise of inflation rates in the North, sometimes to historic peaks, created or aided the growth of several negative pressures — extending from the policy level to that of structural change — that were later to assure a much more deflationary response to the second oil crisis. Thus inflation rates in most leading industrial countries surpassed 15 per cent per annum in 1974, while inflation rates in 1980, after the second oil crisis, were considerably lower, and have now dropped to very low levels.[23] The integration of Northern economies — despite the short upsurge in exports to the South, which only partially reversed long-term trends — quickly transmitted inflation from country to country, but only slowly to developing countries. In many developed countries not previously accustomed to high inflation, such as the United States, West Germany, Switzerland, and the United Kingdom, it is easy to argue that 'imported inflation' (whether, in fact, imported or not) quickly became a political issue, leading to the emergence of harsh, even simplistic, deflationary policies. No better example of this exists than the monetarist policies of the United Kingdom under Mrs Thatcher, and of the United States under President Reagan.

The finance policies under the 'new monetarism' and 'supply-side economies' have now certainly beaten inflation. But in achieving this, interest rates were driven to post-1945 peaks during 1981–2, world trade has declined, and commodity prices have reached a twenty-year low. Country after country in the higher-income developing world has experienced a mounting debt crisis, and the North is now having to face the highest unemployment rates in decades. It is difficult to describe this concurrence of negative factors as 'adjustment' in any meaningful and positive sense.

Although this picture is fragmented, and evolving rapidly, the following firm conclusions clearly emerge. (Yet others can be offered, but these are not such that one can be reasonably certain of their strong deterministic character.) For the industrialising South, as well as the poorer developing countries, the current economic recession is almost certainly the worst ever experienced. As the country profiles in subsequent chapters will show, many of the poorer and several of the middle-income developing countries have, in the period of this study, drifted towards expediency, political repression, and the loss of national pride. The sample countries selected for study have in no way escaped this 'erosion', which is either due to, or accelerated by, stagnation and impoverishment. The South must of course shoulder its share of the blame, but so too must the North, through its economic recovery. It is to be hoped that this conclusion will be understood by more leaders in the

North, and that deflationary, restrictive, and small-minded economic policies — which are severely damaging the North as well as the South — will be quickly superseded by those of benefit to all.

Notes

1. I.F.I. Shihata, 'Inter-South co-operation . . .', in *8th Roundtable Conference on Energy and Economic Development,* Zagreb, Institute for Developing Countries, October 1980.
2. 'UNO, un seul monde', *Le Monde,* issue on UN food programme, 7 October 1980.
3. IBRD, *World Development Report,* New York, Oxford University Press, 1981, p. 53.
4. Presented in very broad, aggregate figures; these are further broken down in following chapters, for sample countries.
5. ICIDI, *North–South: A Programme for Survival,* London, Pan Books, 1980, pp. 224–36.
6. IBRD, *World Development Report,* 1981, p. 52.
7. The 'Lombard rate' is the London Interbank Offer Rate (LIBOR), the basic minimum inter-bank finance cost.
8. A. Angelini *et al., International Lending Risk and the Euromarkets,* London, Macmillan, 1979.
9. The IBRD *World Development Report* of 1981, for example, presents the projection that South–South trade will grow from 27 to 32 per cent of all Southern exports in the period 1980–90. However, it also notes that industrial exports from the South are unlikely to take more than 5 per cent of the Northern market by 1990.
10. S. Mukherjee and C. Feller, *Restructuring of Industrial Economies and Trade with Developing Countries,* Geneva, ILO-BIT, 1981.
11. B. Balassa, 'The changing international division of labour in manufactured goods', IBRD Working Paper 329, Washington DC, IBRD, 1979.
12. G. Renshaw, *Employment Growth and Basic Needs, A One-World Problem* (2nd edn.), Geneva, ILO, 1978, Section 3.
13. D. Nelson, 'The political structure of the new protectionism', World Bank Staff Working Paper No. 471, Washington DC, IBRD, 1981.
14. B. Herman, *The Optimal International Division of Labour,* Geneva, ILO, 1975.
15. IBRD, *World Development Report,* 1981, pp. 68–9.
16. 'La Corée à la recherche d'une nouvelle croissance', Paris, *Le Monde,* 9 October 1982.

17. *Le Monde, Bilan économique et social 1981,* Paris, *Le Monde,* 1981.
18. Ibid.
19. G. de Carmoy, 'The new French energy policy', *Energy Policy,* 10/**3**, September 1982.
20. EEC, 'Energy issue', *EEC-ACP Courier,* **51**, September-October 1978.
21. Bank of England, *Quarterly Bulletin,* various issues.
22. *Financial Times,* London, 1 April 1981.
23. 'Inflation and growth', *Financial Times,* London, 25 June 1982.

3 THE CASE STUDIES

3.1 Introduction

This chapter analyses the responses of the six sample developing countries (chosen at random) to the first and second oil crises. In many ways these six countries (Bangladesh, Sri Lanka, Kenya, Senegal, Peru, Jamaica) are representative of all developing countries — if, in fact, there can be any such thing as an 'average' developing country. About 20 per cent of the developing world's 3.3 billion people in 1980 lived in oil-exporting countries, of which only four were Capital Surplus Oil Exporters with populations above 1 million each. Some eight developing countries — mostly newly industrialising countries — imported over 70 per cent[1] of all the oil taken by the South, which itself uses about 12 per cent of world energy, and imports about 16 per cent of world oil imports.

The countries studied here are part of a group of about 111 developing countries which import about 4 per cent of world oil demands. Depending on whether India is classified as a newly industrialised country or as a poor developing country (because of its low income per capita), the population of this large group of developing countries is about 1,200 million, or 1,850 million if India is included. Of the developing countries, some thirty-one are classified as the poorest or 'most seriously affected' (MSA). In our sample, Bangladesh is in this category. Such countries, it should be noted, have an energy crisis far more basic than that connected with commerical fuels such as oil. This fundamental energy crisis is seen in the erosion of land, the loss of land to desert, and wasted human effort in collecting wood, dung, and crop wastes for cooking fuel.

Most of the sample countries show important similarities with countries in the same income group, apart from Sri Lanka, which has relatively high-level social conditions for its income and growth performance. The two low-income countries, Kenya and Senegal, have much lower life expectancy and literacy rates than Sri Lanka, despite having a much higher GNP per capita. The two remaining sample countries are at the higher end of the income spectrum for middle-income countries. While one (Jamaica) has shown very poor economic progress throughout the 1970s, the other (Peru) became an oil exporter after 1978, but without solving its financial, trade, and other development problems. In all the sample countries, the erosion of earning power through gradually (or rapidly) weakening terms of trade, linked to non-oil primary exports, has been a major negative factor, although since 1979–80 oil exports have eliminated the current account deficit problem for Peru.

Although the sample in this study was drawn at random, the countries have shown many similarities in economic, financial, energy, and development experience throughout the period.

3.1.1 Methodology of country analysis

In this and the following chapters (4 to 8 inclusive), the approach is to isolate the factors that appear to have a significant bearing on the economic development performance of the countries studied. For the purpose of analysis, this chapter is divided into six sections:

(i) a country study of each sample country relative to all developing countries, and relative to poorer developing countries and middle-income developing countries (classified according to income group);
(ii) economic and trade factors throughout the study period;
(iii) finance and debt factors;
(iv) energy trends;
(v) social and economic development; and
(vi) special factors, unique to the countries in the sample.

3.1.2 Study of each sample country relative to all developing countries

This analysis uses the normative analysis of Chenery *et al.*,[2] in which some 100 countries were analysed by their stage of development, judged by various performance criteria, throughout the period 1950–70. The results of this analysis include the classification of socio-economic indicators by GNP per capita — for example the percentage of GNP of industrial origin, investment as a percentage of GNP, and so on. This provides the basis for a comparison of the performance of countries in various fields of economic activity. To this data is added the performance of each country, in each selected indicator, in the years 1978–79. The analysis of this composite data gives the variations in each indicator over time and across countries.

3.1.3 Economic and trade factors

Certain economic — and more especially trade — factors vital to a country's performance, and their capacity for adjustment in the sample countries, are selected and treated. These are itemised and discussed in Section 3.3.

3.1.4 Finance and debt factors

In Chapters 1 and 2 it was established that these variables differed significantly throughout the oil crisis and recovery periods. This sector of the analysis, therefore, isolates certain factors, detailed in Section 3.4, for furhter investigation. The bulk of the data used for this analysis is from IBRD and official sources, standardised wherever possible. The data are presented mainly in tables, but in certain cases in graphs.

3.2 Study of each sample country relative to all developing countries

As already indicated, this section uses the analyses of over 100 developing — and some developed — countries throughout the period 1950–70, as presented by Chenery *et al.* In the work cited,[3] a large number of economic variables, termed 'accumulation processes', are used for analysis, including: three investment variables; two government revenue variables; two education variables; three domestic variables; four production share variables; five production structure variables; five trade variables; and eight variables related to socio-economic structure, including urbanisation. From these, this study utilises the following five variables for further treatment:

1 share of industry in GNP;
2 dependence on primary product exports;
3 share of services in GNP;
4 investment as a share of GDP; and
5 share of labour force in agriculture.

Progression As can be seen from the analysis by Chenery *et al.*, the variation in these five variables, according to GNP per capita, is often about 200 to 300 per cent from the lowest- to the highest-income countries. These variables are therefore significant development indicators.

Economic exposure The chosen indicators, particularly those relating to industry's share of GNP and to primary product exports dependence, indicate to what extent the sample countries are affected by external economic factors, such as terms of trade.

Energy Many of the chosen variables, notably the service sector's share of GNP (reflective of infrastructure level and urbanisation), and industry's share of GNP, exert significant influence on the commercial energy demands of the economy.

3.2.1 Disaggregation of chosen variables

1 *Share of industry in GNP* This bears a close relationship to the need for investment, and also to the demand for commercial energy, since the establishment and operation of industrial plant, transport, services, etc., are commercial energy dependent.

2 *Dependence on primary product exports* The analysis by Chenery *et al.* shows that concentration of exports in the primary sector falls off quite rapidly as GNP increases, and as industry's share of GNP increases, etc. Where the commodities concerned are relatively energy-intensive, notably minerals and metals, adverse terms of trade movements for the minerals and metals concerned can lead to additional economic and financial problems.

3 *Share of services in GNP* The share of the service sector in GNP cannot grow until significant urbanisation, and some industrialisation, has taken place. Thus the growth of services is a development-related activity. Once this growth has taken place, a commitment to expanded commercial energy use becomes established in the economy.

4 *Investment as a share of GDP* Chenery *et al.* demonstrated that investment levels increase rapidly once certain thresholds of GNP per capita are reached. Since investment is particularly oriented to the 'modern sector', the growth of investment will again have major implications for commercial energy demand.

5 *Share of labour force in agriculture* This again has significant impacts on the prospective growth of demand, since the growth of labour used *outside* the agricultural sector implies its use in highly capitalised, more commerical energy dependent economic sectors.

3.2.2 Treatment and interpretation of data

As shown in Table 3.1, the six sample countries fall within four of the income per capita groups used by Chenery *et al.* For each of these income groups, using data from Chenery *et al.* updated to 1978–9 US dollars, the following are shown:

(i) classification of over 100 countries by income per capita;
(ii) average score for that country group, per chosen variable, in 1950-70;
(iii) score for the sample country, in 1978–9, for that chosen variable; and
(iv) deviation from the 1950–70 average.

The performance of the six sample countries is shown n Table 3.1 and Figure 1, using the five chosen economic indicators.

Share of industry in GNP In this sector it is noticeable that only Sri Lanka has a very large variation (+108 per cent) from its similar-income country group's average for the period 1950–70. Thus, although Sri Lanka has been described by certain development institutions[4] as a country that '... chose investments in human and social progres rather than economic growth', its industrial growth was still substantial.

The scores for Bangladesh, Kenya, and Senegal are within 15 per cent of the 1950–70 average for their respective similar-income group of countries, thus indicating little industrial growth from the averages for 1950–70, right through to 1979. In the case of Sri Lanka, the period from approximately 1973–8 was marked by an increase in import-substituting industries[5] which, due to industrial structure, were not particularly constrained by capital availability. On the other hand, in Senegal, and certainly in Kenya,[6] the trend of industrialisation — which was not dynamic — was towards relatively capital-intensive, and therefore energy-intensive, systems. This has had important effects on relative oil import demands and growth throughout the period.

The two highest-income sample countries (Peru and Jamaica) show some increase in industrial activity in 1978–9, relative to the

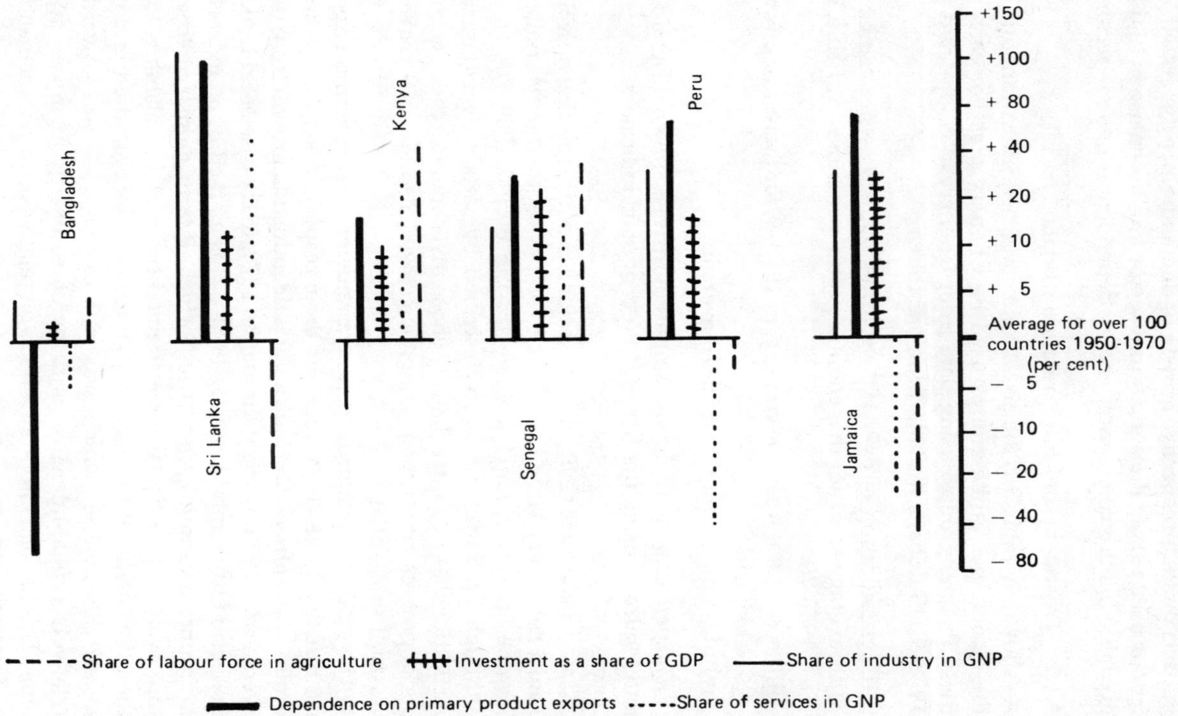

Fig 3.1 Each sample country's performance in five chosen variables for 1978–1979 relative to performance averages for over 100 countries in the period 1950–1970*

Table 3.1 Each sample country's performance in five chosen variables for 1978–1979 relative to performance averages for over 100 countries in the period 1950–1970 (after Chenery ***et al.***)*

Country group	*Performance in country group average for 1950–70*				
	Share of industry in GNP (per cent)	*Dependence on primary product exports (as a percentage of GDP)*	*Share of services in GNP (per cent)*	*Investment as a share of GDP per cent per annum*	*Share of labour force in agriculture (per cent)*
Country GNP/capita group, 1978–9 average ($US of GNP/capita)					
Countries under $US 100 GNP/capita	0.125	0.130	0.300	0.136	0.712
Bangladesh	0.130	0.035	0.305	0.130	0.740
Variation (per cent)	+4	−76	+1.6	−4.5	+4
Countries of $US 100–200 GNP/capita	0.149	0.137	0.338	0.158	0.658
Sri Lanka	0.310	0.281	0.380	0.240	0.540
Variation (per cent)	+108	+101	+12	+52	−17
Countries of $US 200–400 GNP/capita	0.215	0.136	0.385	0.188	0.557
A *Kenya*	0.200	0.158	0.425	0.250	0.785
Variation (per cent)	−7	+16.2	+10.4	+33	+41
B *Senegal*	0.245	0.183	0.480	0.220	0.767
Variation (per cent)	+14	+34.5	+24.6	+17	+37.5
Countries of $US 1,000–1,600 GNP/capita	0.294	0.120	0.415	0.220	0.396
A *Peru*	0.395	0.212	0.485	0.145	0.385
Variation (per cent)	+34.5	+76.7	+17	−34	−2.5
B *Jamaica*	0.395	0.214	0.525	0.165	0.220
Variation (per cent)	+34.5	+78.3	+26.5	−25	−44.3

* The data in Chenery *et al.* (*Patterns of Development*, Oxford, Oxford University Press, 1975), use 1964 $US, and these have been converted using IBRD data. Country scores and the scores for 1950–70, for each variable, are shown as fractions (e.g. 0.395 = 39.5 per cent) in order to highlight percentage variations from long-run averages (percentage variation columns).

1950–70 group average. Nevertheless, their record of growth is most certainly not comparable with countries such as South Korea or Malaysia, which in the 1960s had similar or inferior levels of per capita income. Peru and Jamaica have maintained inward-looking, import-substituting industrialisation policies, unlike the newly industrialised developing countries.

2 *Dependence on primary product exports* Several countries in the sample show very large variations from their respective similar-income group's average for 1950–70. In Bangladesh, the classification of jute-procesing as 'industrial' greatly reduces the country's score in this second category, but in fact Bangladesh is extremely dependent on jute and other agricultural soft commodities, and 98 per cent of its exports in 1978–9 were of three primary products.[7] During the period 1961–70 Sri Lanka was also extremely dependent on primary exports, in this instance tea, gems, and certain other plantation crops (for example spices). While these products are not energy-intensive in fuel input/market price output terms, they are sensitive to terms of trade variations. Commodity prices are in turn affected by international economic trends, such as post-oil crisis recessions, instability of markets, and so forth. Similar factors apply to Kenya (which exports coffee, tea, and pyrethrum) and to Senegal (which exports peanuts). Both countries have been greatly affected by terms of trade movements.

Peru and Jamaica, despite their higher incomes, are also very dependent on primary product exports. These are not soft commodities, but copper (Peru) and aluminium ore (Jamaica), and certain other non-oil minerals. Additionally, in the case of Jamaica there was, until the late 1970s, an important sugar-cane industry. Other than sugar-cane, all these activities are energy-intensive, and all (including sugar-cane) are very sensitive to terms of trade and to the performance of the North.

3 *Share of services in GNP* As previously noted, the growth of the service sector is dependent on both urbanisation and industrialisation, and implies a continuous increase in demand. This is seen in its most intense form in the Arab states where, with increased GNP and commercial use, the service sector of the economy has expanded enormously in short periods of time. Relative to their respective similar-income group's average for 1950–70, only Senegal and Jamaica record large increases in the service sector in 1978–9. It

could be that the combination of smallness of size, primary orientation (non-oil commodities), and geographical isolation of the sample countries has not favoured growth in the service sector. In the cases of Senegal and Jamaica, it could be argued that Senegal's important ex-administrative role in Francophone, West Africa, and Jamaica's large tourist industry, have aided these countries' service growth.

The relatively low growth in service industries in Bangladesh, Sri Lanka, and Kenya is significant. The low growth rates of service industries in Bangladesh can be explained by the 1971–2 war, coupled with poverty.[8] In Sri Lanka, however, the explanation may lie in the country's import-substituting industrialisation policies. Until 1976–8, services and export-oriented industries were discouraged, partly because of the outflow of skilled service industry workers.[9] In Kenya, unlike Sri Lanka, the relatively low level or urbanisation (only 14 per cent of the population in 1980) and the low population density, coupled with geographical remoteness, may be important reasons for the low levels of service growth relative to the 1950–70 group average.

4 *Investment as a share of GDP* Apart from Sri Lanka, and Kenya to a much smaller extent, the sample countries do not show significant progress in comparison with the 1950–70 group averages. Lack of investment, coupled with the highly competitive world market scene that developed in the 1970s (due notably to rapid export increases by many newly industrialised countries) led to or heightened the problem of slow industrial growth and continued high dependence on primary product exports in the sample countries.

Apart from Bangladesh, and to a much greater extent Sri Lanka,[10] all the sample countries recorded quite high relative inflows of capital throughout the period. Thus consumption increases could utilise internal increments of wealth to a higher level than that (about 50 per cent) found to be typical for all developing countries over Chenery's study period.[11] On the other hand, Sri Lanka suffered from shortages of foreign capital inflows around the mid-1960s, which may have encouraged investment rather than consumption.

The relatively low levels of investment are especially marked in Peru and Jamaica. Whatever the political background (which has been clearly evoked for Jamaica by the policies of the Manley governments[12] and by the IMF,[13] though each from very different stances), the country had very low rates of savings throughout the 1970s. This was made much more severe by net outflows of capital in certain years. Similar, but less severe problems affected Peru throughout the study period.

5 *Share of labour force in agriculture* Apart from Sri Lanka and Jamaica, the other countries in the sample record high proportionate levels of agricultural labour in relation to GNP. Despite this, most of these countries became quite large food importers throughout the study period, but because of constant or decreasing real food prices in world markets most have not needed to make large increases in foreign exchange outflows in order to assure food import needs.

The composition of agricultural activity, especially in Kenya and Senegal, has tended to discourage food production and to encourage export-oriented crops. Bangladesh, for example, has the worst food problems of the sample countries because development policies have either ignored agriculture or actively discouraged it.[14] This has been a recurrent problem in certain African and Latin American countries.[15] Peru, with an urban population of about 70 per cent of the total population, has acute food supply problems, despite very large land resources.

It is noticeable, also, that the effects of national policy tend to magnify with time. Thus Jamaica's pursuit of industrial and manufacturing development has led to it having the lowest agricultural labour percentage recorded in the sample. Yet Sri Lanka, with a similar population density, has a much higher level of agricultural labour, and does not have such large food import costs and logistic problems.

3.2.3 Summary of sample-country characteristics for 1978–9, relative to the averages for 100-odd countries in 1950–70

The preceding analysis of selected characteristics as shown by each of the sample countries is outlined in Table 3.2, which summarises the factors which are potentially most important for economic adjustment.

3.3 Economic factors in the process of adjustment

The role of economic forces in adjustment is critical. Therefore,

Table 3.2 Sample-country characteristics, a summary

Factor	*Bangladesh*	*Sri Lanka*	*Kenya*	*Senegal*	*Peru*	*Jamaica*
Share of industry in GNP	AV	VHI ‡	LO †	AAV	AAV	HI
Dependence on primary product exports	HI*	VHI*†	HI*†	AAV*	VHI*	VHI*
Share of servics in GNP	AV	AV	AV	AAV	AAV	HI*
Investment as a share of GDP	AV	HI ‡	AAV	AAV	LO*	LO*
Share of labour force in agriculture	AAV †	AV	VHI	AAV †	AV	LO †

Symbols: AV: average; AAV: above average; HI: high; LO: low; VHI: very high; * potential direct adjustment problem factor; † indirect problem factor; ‡ adjustment factor.

using a large range of data sources, this section reviews and analyses those which appear to be most important. Because of the diversity of sources, it is again important to note the problem relating to the reliability and consistency of data. In most cases, data from UN agencies, and from IBRD, IMF, and official country sources are used. However, because the period 1973–80 was marked by such unprecedented economic change, high inflation, and rapid fluctuations in the value of the US dollar, it must be appreciated that there is considerable scope for error.

After reviewing the major economic factors, this section presents an analysis of how these factors have tended to assist, or hinder, the adjustment process. In many cases this raises questions of theory and interpretation, which are considered further in Chapters 4 to 7.

3.3.1 Basic economic characteristics

As shown in Table 3.3, the sample countries fall into three main IBRD income groups, and into four of the five categories of non-OPEC developing countries used in analysis by the Brookhaven National Laboratory (BNL).to some extent the BNL analysis, which uses the United Nations Standard Industrial Classification system, is too exclusive. In particular, it should be noted that Kenya and Bangladesh (Group Va) are separated from Senegal and Sri Lanka (Group Vb) on the basis of industrial classification. However, these four countries share more similarities than differences, especially in relation to their export composition.

Table 3.3 Basic economic characteristics of the sample countries, 1970–1979

Country	*Area (1,000 sq. km.)*	*Population density (persons per sq. km.) 1979*	*Population growth rate (annual average per cent) 1970-9*	*GNP per capita 1979 (in 1979 $US dollars)*	*GDP 1979 (in $US billions at 1979 prices)*	*IBRD income group*	*BNL developing country group**	*Potential NPP† (million tons per year)*	*Potential NPP† per person 1979 (tons/capita)*
Bangladesh	144	617	3.0	90	7.67	MSA‡	Group Vb	347	6.5
Sri Lanka	66	220	1.7	230	3.16	Low-income	Group Va	100	7.5
Kenya	239	64	3.4	380	5.28	Middle-income	Group Vb	412	35
Senegal	197	28	2.6	430	2.3	Middle-income	Group Va	210	50
Peru	1,286	14	2.7	730	14.7	Middle-income	Group III	1,871	125
Jamaica	11	200	1.6	1,260	2.39	Middle-income	Group IV	19	10

* BNL developing country categories are: Group III, 'balanced growth' economies, described as having significant industry with a continuing, important agricultural component, and dependent on imported energy for over 50 per cent of their needs; Group IV, 'primary exporters', where mineral exports are important, and the countries are over 50 per cent dependent on energy imports; Group Va, 'agricultural-oriented' countries which are dependent on soft-commodity exports; Group Vb is similar, but less dependent on such exports; both groups are import-dependent for over 50 per cent of their energy requirements.

† See Section 3.3.1 for a discussion of NPP.

‡ MSA — most seriously affected.

Sources: IBRD, *World Development Report,* New York, Oxford University Press, 1980, 1981; UNESCAP, 'Development Strategies in the 1980s in the ESCAP region', *ad hoc* inter-governmental meeting on strategies for the 1980s, Bangkok, UNESCAP, August 1979; Brookhaven National Laboratory, *Energy Needs and Resources in Developing Countries,* New York, BNL, 1978; and S.R. Eyre, *The Real Wealth of Nations,* London, Arnold, 1978.

The last two columns of Table 3.3. show net productivity potential in million tons and per capita respectively.[16] This concept, developed by S. Eyre and others, is used here to indicate the maximum potential yield of a country's land mass under optimum management, and to express this (final column) as the maximum possible yield per capita of organic products of all kinds. Few coun tries in the OECD could hope to approach even 50 per cent of their net productivity potential (NPP) yield (because of environmental damage, mismanagement, etc.), but many developing countries are actually now seriously damaging their environments without achieving large increases in GNP growth rates.

Data treating NPP and NPP per capita for 1979[17] show that Bangladesh and Sri Lanka have scores similar to such countries as Lebanon, Hong Kong, Burundi, Rwanda, and Taiwan. Of these, only those countries which have diversified in both the industrial and the service sector have shown real economic development. While no single factor can explain lack of development, it is signifi cant that the development opportunities of the two poorest countries have been constrained by land shortage.

The income per capita for the sample countries is, apart from Jamaica, quite low. This supports the argument that all the sample countries in this study are 'dependent' on the world economy and world economic trends. As will be seen, many have suffered large reversals of economic fortune throughout the study period, with quite large contractions of GDP in certain years. Geographically, the sample group is split between the land-rich countries of Peru, Kenya, and Senegal (which can be included in this category as a result of much capital-intensive land improvement, notably irrigation), and the other three land-poor countries.

3.3.2 GDP trends during the study period

Gross Domestic Product (GDP) at constant market prices (national currency prices) has been chosen as the major analytic variable in this section for the following reasons:

(i) GDP minus factor payments to the rest of the world (r.o.w.) gives a good indication of internal economic performance;
(ii) expressed in national currencies, GDP figures limit currency equivalence problems;[18] and
(iii) GDP figures eliminate the factor of ODA and other variable inflows of capital.

The data presented in Table 3.4 are derived mainly from the IBRD *World Tables,*[19] using data expressed in national currencies at certain fixed prices. These data are then supplemented by IBRD data from various *World Development Reports,*[20] and by official country data. It has been found that the data in the IBRD *World Tables* are usually expressed in calendar terms, avoiding the problems implicit in the treatment of fiscal year data using different time bases, such as those used by the IMF.[21] This is particularly important for evaluating foreign exchange outflows for oil imports, since in IMF data for certain countries (including Bangladesh and Sri Lanka in this sample) the increased outflows for oil purchases (following the price rises of November 1973 to March 1974) are only shown in the financial year 1975.

It is of course regretted that expressing GDP in national currency terms, rather than in US dollars, in Table 3.4 prevents a quick appreciation of the size and variation of GDP for each country in the study period. However, GDP growth rates are known (and analysed in the following sections), and where necessary IBRD data on national GDP in US dollars have been used.

3.3.3 GDP Performance and the 'central hypothesis'

The data presented in Table 3.4 can be interpreted in ways which both support and controvert this hypothesis. Apart from Banglad esh (which is a very special case, due notably to the war of independence in 1971), some of the sample countries, particularly Senegal and Jamaica, experienced a *reversal* of GDP growth from 1972 and 1974. On the other hand, Sri Lanka, Kenya, and Peru (still an oil importer in 1972–7) showed distinct *increases* in their GDP growth rates, especially during the period 1973–6, when the crop growth rates were considerably higher than the 1970–2 average. In comparing the performance of the sample countries with the 'economic adjustment models' of the IBRD, one can argue that only one country, Jamaica, showed a significant *decrease* in GDP during the first oil crisis period of 1973–5. And while (as is noted in later chapters) foreign exchange outflows for energy imports rose rapidly as current account deficits increased for all the sample countries, it was only Sri Lanka and Jamaica that recorded major falls in national commercial energy use. Senegal, whose GDP showed a marked decline during 1972–4, showed a significant *rise* in commercial energy imports during this period.

As will be seen in Chapter 6 on energy, the transmission of

Table 3.4 GDP and growth/contraction rates* for each of the sample countries, selected years, 1970–1979

	GDP minus factor payments to abroad							*Annual average per-GDP percentage change*		*per capita*
Country	*1970*	*1972*	*1973*	*1974*	*1975*	*1977*	*1979*	*1970-7*	*1973-7*	*1970-8*
Bangladesh										
Billion taka at 1970 prices	53.69	43.66	45.43	50.28	52.06	58.82	59.80	1.6	4.6	−0.4
Sri Lanka										
Billion rupees at 1959 prices	10.69	11.15	11.50	11.73	12.05	12.89	14.85	2.9	4.2	2.0
Kenya										
Billion shillings at 1972 prices	12.92	14.43	15.43	16.09	16.20	18.42	20.55	5.2	4.9	2.2
Senegal										
Billion CFA francs at 1971 prices	247.00	263.00	248.00	259.00	283.00	291.00	308.50	2.4	3.6	−0.2
Peru										
Billion soles at 1963 prices	114.90	127.10	134.90	144.20	149.00	151.70	155.50	4.0	2.4	1.4
Jamaica										
Billion $Jam. at 1974 prices	2,019	2,260	2,259	2,265	2,244	2,011	1,710	−0.1	−4.5	−1.9

* Measured in GDP minus factor payments to abroad at constant market prices, in named currency units.

Sources: IBRD, *World Tables*, Baltimore, Johns Hopkins University Press, 1980, 1981; and IBRD, *World Development Report*, 1980, 1981.

energy price rises to the economy of a developing country involves two main factors, product mix, and price policies. Thus countries such as Jamaica, where heavy products form an important part of consumption, experienced much *smaller* price rises over the 1973–5 period, relative to countries where lighter products supply most demand. Yet Jamaica experienced a large decrease in energy demand during the study period, and also experienced a decline in GDP. Consequently, alternative factors, such as terms of trade and demand for major exports, must be sought to explain why the IBRD model of developing country oil price economic adjustment has not been realised in the six sample countries. Furthermore, the 'conventional hypothesis' defines adjustment as increased domination of the internal market, and better penetration of external markets. This concept of adjustment is opposed by structural factors, such as small markets and weak industrialisation, which were found to be strong in at least four, even five, of the sample countries. As indicated in Table 3.3, only Peru can be depicted as a Group III 'balanced growth' economy, that is, one in which there is significant industrial change. Even here, and certainly in Jamaica's case, the development of industry has been constrained by economic (dominance of mineral exports), geographical (small, rather remote, and internally dispersed markets), and 'scale of the market' factors. In all the other sample countries with the exception of Sri Lanka, the combination of economic, geographical, and scale factors, coupled with a low GNP per capita base and rapid population growth, has made adjustment through industrial expansion a very different option. However, price rises, which affected not only oil but also consumer and capital goods import prices (shown in the overall downward drift in terms of trade and other factors), have encouraged industrialisation policies.

It was in accord with the last adjustment category of the IBRD (additional real financing) that *all* of the sample countries responded to the first oil crisis, but evidence on what is happening in the slow world recovery from the 1979 oil crisis is still not clear. In terms of additional inflows relative to GDP, some countries borrowed new capital from around 1973–5. The period of advantageous terms of trade movements (approximately 1975–7), however short, also helped to bring about markedly higher GDP growth rates in the period 1973 to 1976–7, relative to averages for the decade. At least three of the sample countries were clearly in this category.

3.4 Trade and terms of trade

Throughout the study period all the sample countries, with one exception, showed overall increases in trade deficits as a percentage of GNP, although national incomes had grown, for four out of the six countries, by around 130 to 150 per cent in real terms during 1970–9. There was, also, an increasing *convergence* of trends towards trade deficits, despite great changes in the volume and direction of trade.

The data for this analysis of trade flows for the sample countries are presented in Table 3.5. From these data it is possible to identify some general trends, which are presented in Table 3.6. Figure 3.2 illustrates the trade trends of the sample countries throughout the study period. As can be seen from Table 3.5 and Figure 3.2, there were important changes in the economic climates of many of the sample countries throughout the decade 1970–80. External economic factors, and widespread (often global) economic changes, made this decade a period of discontinuity and rapid change.

It can be seen from Table 3.6 that the trade data indicate at least four different periods, or groups of trade years, in which all or most of the sample countries experienced similar events. In period (3), for example, there was great buoyancy of nearly all the sample countries, with trade gaps narrowing radically, and three countries recording a surplus in 1977. This was just twelve to eighteen months after the first oil crisis, and it is obvious, therefore, that higher-priced oil had not destroyed the trade prospects for most of these countries. In 1980, the OECD Northern countries' economic activity picked up, following the lead of newly industrialised countries such as South Korea and Brazil. The latter's economic growth came directly after the first round of oil price rises, as petrodollars were recycled through trade. This external buoyancy maintained the terms of trade, which (as will be seen) was perhaps the most important trade factor for the sample countries.

Although the sample countries span a large range of GNP per capita (there is approximately an eighteenfold gap between the GNP per capita of Jamaica and that of Bangladesh), and although some countries, notably Sri Lanka, have invested in industry, the role of primary product exports has been paramount in deciding trade balances for all the sample countries. This trend has certainly become stronger, not weaker, throughout the study period. Although Figure 3.2 shows that there were quite large variations in

Table 3.5 Visible trade surplus (+) or deficit for each sample country as a percentage of GNP, selected years, 1970–1979 (current $US throughout)

Country/factor	*1970*	*1972*	*1973*	*1974*	*1975*	*1976*	*1977*	*1978*	*1979*
Bangladesh									
GNP ($US billions)	n/a*	n/a	5.89	8.23	11.48	6.72	6.18	7.55	7.67
Trade deficit ($US millions)	n/a	n/a	393	645	843	384	563	720	691
Deficit as percentage of GNP	—	—	6.8	7.8	7.3	5.7	9.1	9.8	11.1
Sri Lanka									
GNP ($US billions)	1.85	1.83	1.98	2.51	2.64	2.41	2.34	2.71	3.30
Trade deficit ($US millions)	14	6	5	120	20	+102	+98	93	467
Deficit as percentage of GNP	0.1	0	0	4.8	0.08	+4.2	+4.2	3.4	14.2
Kenya									
GNP ($US billions)	1.54	1.96	2.24	2.73	3.04	3.28	4.26	4.85	5.81
Trade deficit ($US millions)	87	117	75	317	224	62	+13	687	534
Deficit as percentage of GNP	5.6	6.0	3.3	11.6	7.4	1.9	+0.3	14.0	9.2
Senegal									
GNP ($US billions)	0.84	1.06	1.22	1.36	1.84	1.88	n/a	1.84	2.3
Trade deficit ($US millions)	45	59	161	136	108	146	n/a	397	330
Deficit as percentage of GNP	5.3	5.6	7.6	10.0	5.9	12.9	n/a	21.6	14.2
Peru									
GNP ($US billions)	6.08	7.49	9.10	11.34	13.31	13.02	12.20	12.43	12.48
Trade deficit ($US millions)	+335	+133	+15	404	1,098	740	438	11	+1,384
Deficit as percentage of GNP	+5.5	+1.8	+0.0	3.6	12.1	5.7	3.6	0.0	+11.1
Jamaica									
GNP ($US billions)	1.34	2.73	1.89	2.43	2.82	2.89	3.1	2.33	2.77
Trade deficit ($US millions)	108	152	178	59	161	132	+93	162	241
Deficit as percentage of GNP	8.1	5.6	9.4	2.4	5.7	4.6	+2.9	6.9	8.6

* n/a — no available data.

Sources: IBRD, *World Tables,* 1980; IBRD, *World Development Report,* 1980, 1981; and official sources.

Table 3.6 Generalised trade trends for the sample countries throughout the study period*

Period	*Trend in trade and trade deficits*	*Probable/likely reasons*
(1) 1969–72	Tendency for stability in trade of sample countries. Significant growth in exports. Exception: Peru.	Buoyant world markets. Fast fall of trade surplus, rapid imports growth.
(2) 1972–4/5	Period of rapid change, following first oil crisis. Kenya, Sri Lanka, Senegal: very fast rises in trade deficits, but reversed equally rapidly. Bangladesh: stabilised, high deficits. Peru: very fast-rising deficits. Jamaica: initial fast fall of deficits, followed by rapid increases.	Oil crisis, OECD countries' recession. Improving trade terms for exports after 1973–4. Declining trade terms. Imports growth; decline in trade terms. Contraction of economy; trade terms rise, then fall.
(3) 1875–7	All countries except Senegal and Bangladesh show very rapid decrease in trade deficits (three show surpluses). Peru: dramatic reversal of deficits. Senegal: increasing deficits, at slowed rate of increase. Bangladesh: increasing deficits.	OECD countries' recovery/growth. Improved trade terms. Increased capital inflows. Rapid build-up of oil input. Trade terms, climate problems. Trade terms, political unrest, falling food output.
(4) 1977/8–80	All countries except Senegal and Bangladesh: reversal of trade surpluses, move to deficits bigger than in period (2). Senegal and Bangladesh: slight decrease in deficits, from very high levels. (Peru: oil exporter)	OECD countries' recession. Terms of trade movements. Increased industrial imports Contraction of economy. Stabilised trade terms.

* Based on data shown in Table 3.5.

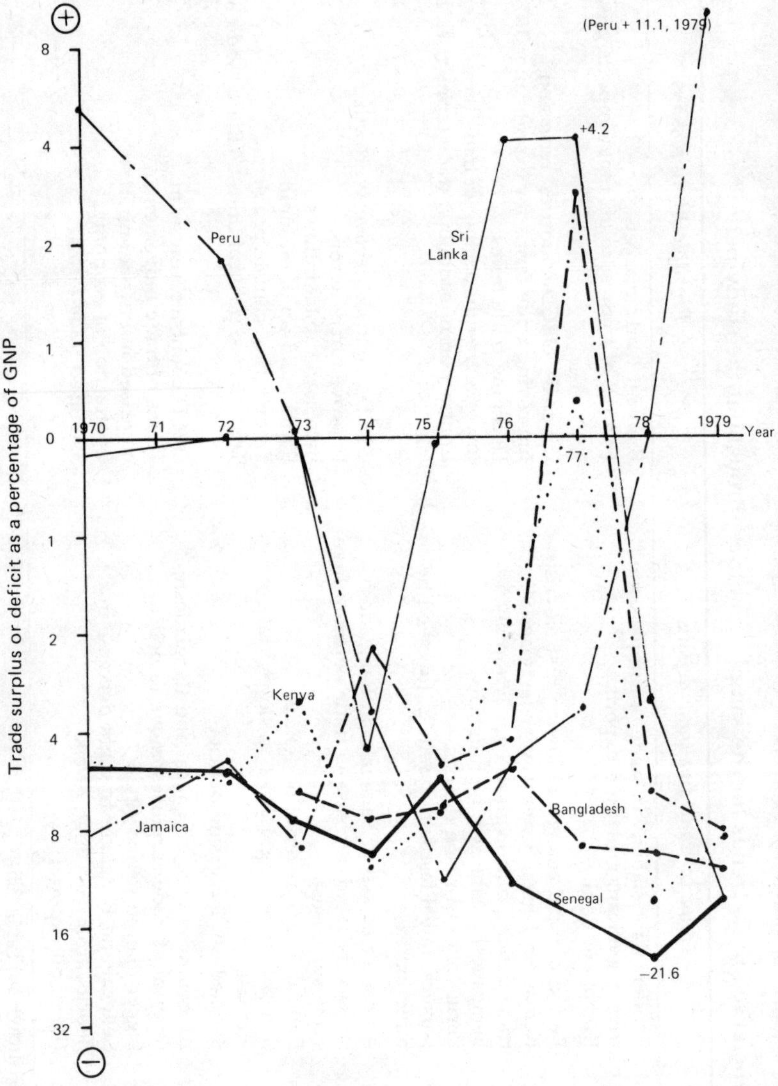

Fig. 3.2 Visible trade surplus or deficit for each sample country as a percentage of GNP, 1970–1979*

* *Based on data shown in Table 3.5*

trade patterns, trade deficits as a percentage of GNP became much more convergent during 1970–80. While the average deficit for the sample countries in 1970 was 2.73 per cent, with a large standard deviation of 4.8, that for 1979 was 11.46 per cent, with only a 2.4 standard deviation. The 1979 figure excludes Peru, which as an oil-exporting developing country cannot be expected to share characteristics common to oil importers, but the 1970 figure includes Peru, as the country was at that time importing oil.

The critical role of the terms of trade and their importance to the sample countries (and to many other developing countries) can be understood from the following:

(i) during the study period several countries, on more than one occasion, experienced swings of more that 30 per cent in their terms of trade; and
(ii) all the countries in the sample are heavily dependent on the export of primary commodities.

Consequently, the OECD countries' rapid recovery after the end of 1975, which quickly shifted the terms of trade in favour of commodities, was most advantageous to several countries in the sample, as is shown by the data presented in Table 3.7. This improvement did not extend to Bangladesh, since world demand for its major export, jute, was at best showing only marginal growth. This is partly explained by the fact that jute can be easily substituted, unlike the major primary products (such as tea, coffee, gems, copper, and bauxite)[22] of the other sample countries. On the other hand, the very poor performance of the two highest-income countries in the sample highlights the particular problem of higher-income (as opposed to lower-income) developing countries. Using IBRD and UN data, the terms of trade variations throughout the study period for all poorer and middle-income developing countries are shown in Figure 3.3. In the 1970s, despite the increasing share of manufactured goods in their total exports, the terms of trade worsened for Peru and Jamaica because the world markets favoured primary products. However, despite their gains due to favourable terms of trade movements, both Kenya and Sri Lanka have accumulated serious current account deficits, requiring more forceful import substitution and industrialisation measures. The same may also be true for Senegal.

As previously noted, only one of the sample countries ended the decade 1970–80 with a trade surplus. This was Peru, for the simple

Table 3.7 Terms of trade and import/export price indices for each sample country, selected years, 1971–1979 (1970 = 100)

Country	*1971*	*1973*	*1974*	*1976*	*1978*	*1979*
Bangladesh						
Import prices	106	146	204	217		
Export prices	104	126	148	156		
Trade terms	98	98	73	72	74	89
Sri Lanka						
Import prices	116	147	225	244		
Export prices	122	150	208	225		
Trade terms	108	102	93	92	112	110
Kenya						
Import prices	108	144	236	265		
Export prices	108	145	212	270		
Trade terms	100	100	90	102	104	100
Senegal						
Import prices	107	146	202	219		
Export prices	114	135	238	242		
Trade terms	107	92	118	110	99	76
Peru						
Import prices	107	144	198	217		
Export prices	91	158	189	176		
Trade terms	85	109	95	81	77	97
Jamaica						
Import prices	107	145	210	232		
Export prices	98	102	175	248		
Trade terms	92	70	83	107	90	93

Sources: IBRD, *World Tables,* 1980; IBRD, *World Development Report,* 1980, 1981; and *Asia and Pacific Annual Review, 1980,* WOI, 1981.

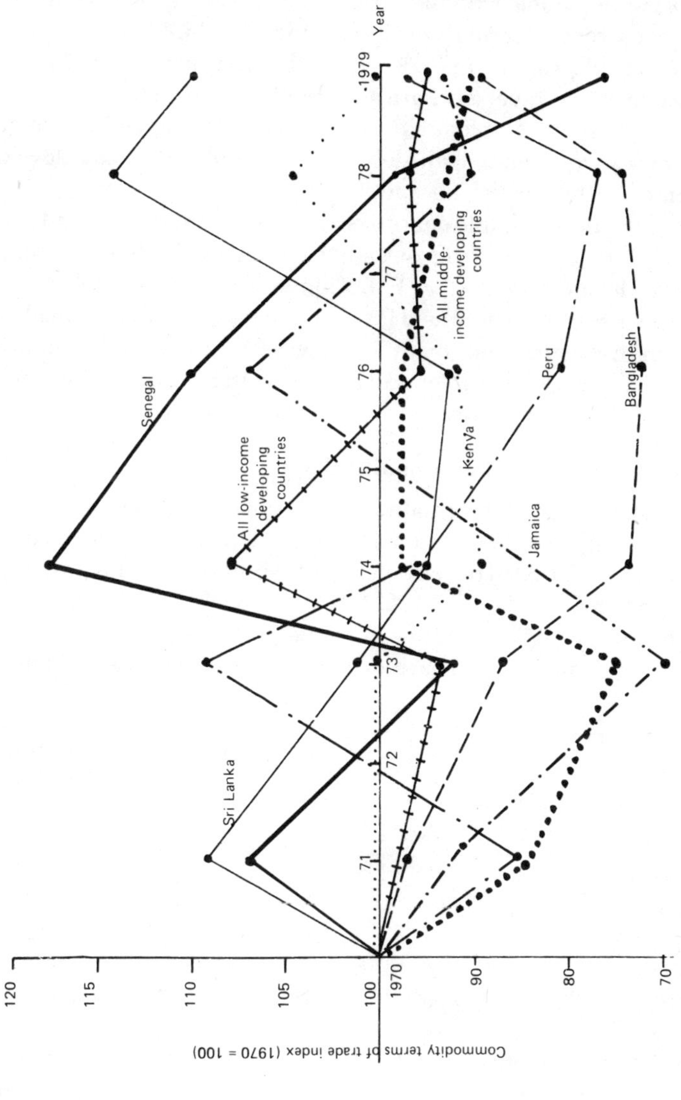

Fig. 3.3 Commodity terms of trade for each sample country, and for all low- and middle-income developing countries, 1970–1979 (1970 = 100)*

* *Based on data shown in Table 3.7*

reason that by late 1978 it had become an oil exporter. Nevertheless, the associated expenditure on oil-related plant and equipment, and on services for field development, had a noticeable impact on Peru's terms of trade and current account deficits during 1973–4. This is comparable with the experience of Norway, which suffered large current account deficits during the build-up period of offshore oil production.[23] However, the accruing wealth from oil has effectively reversed Peru's current account deficit and short-term economic problems. It is possible that, depending on the country's experience with debt management, Peru may develop rapidly in the coming decades.

For the other sample countries, the downward drift — and great variability — of the terms of trade have caused further difficulties. While debate on the UNCTAD Common Fund to stabilise commodity prices has continued for years (leading to a rather small and insignificant fund with many weaknesses),[24] the sample countries have faced serious problems in dealing with the fluctuating market for commodity exports.

3.4.1. Exports and commodity share

The role of primary products in export composition, and the relationship of this factor to GDP, can be gauged from the data presented in Table 3.8. The relationship of exports to GDP for the sample

Table 3.8 GDP, exports as a percentage of GDP, and primary products as a share of exports for each sample country, 1978–1979

Country	*GDP ($US billions)*	*Exports ($US billions)*	*Share of exports in GDP (per cent)*	*Share of primary products in exports (per cent)*
Bangladesh	7.67	0.66	8.6	40.5*
Sri Lanka	3.16	0.98	31.0	90.5
Kenya	5.28	1.10	20.8	88.0
Senegal	2.38	0.42	17.7	93.0
Peru	14.80	3.47	23.2	90.5
Jamaica	2.19	0.77	32.2	66.5

* See Section 3.4.1.

Sources: IBRD, *World Development Report,* 1980, 1981; and IBRD, *World Tables,* 1980.

countries is not, on average, greatly different from that of the industrial countries, but the share of *primary products* exports is very high. While Bangladesh may appear to have achieved exceptional freedom from commodity price pressures according to the low score shown in Table 3.8, this is an illusion based on industrial classification. An examination of the role of jute and jute-based products in Bangladesh's exports (Table 3.9) clearly reveals the marked dependence on jute. Although industrial expansion has been pursued as a major development policy of Sri Lanka, Peru, and Kenya, the reality of these countries' continuing high dependence on primary products is shown quite clearly in Table 3.8.

Table 3.9 Jute, jute-based, and other exports, Bangladesh, 1973–1978 (in crore taka: taka × 10 million)

Exports	*1973–4*	*1974–5*	*1975–6*	*1976–7*	*1977–8*
Raw jute	94.3	75.8	163.4	176.7	154.5
Jute goods	158.7	185.9	277.8	268.1	349.5
All exports	298.3	313.6	555.2	654.1	745.5
Percentage of which jute or jute-based	84.3	83.5	79.5	68.0	67.7

Source: Bangladesh Economic Survey, Dacca, 1979.

The proportion of exports in GDP must be compared with typical rates of exports versus GDP. It is, however, the role of *primary product* exports (where price swings on world markets can be very wide) that differentiates this sample of developing countries from the OECD countries. As a brief illustration of this, exports, GDP, and the primary product export share for a few OECD countries are shown in Table 3.10.

3.4.2 Commodity prices — sugar

The small, relatively open, and overwhelmingly primary-product dependent nations in the sample have a distinct interest in the movement of primary product prices. When these rise, as they did in the period 1972–5, terms of trade move in these countries' favour, thus preserving the earning capacity of their exports. But during the study period the changes in non-oil primary product prices have played havoc with economic forecasting and planning in developing countries such as these.

While it is perhaps an extreme case, sugar demonstrates all the problems facing primary-product export developing countries. These problems have been further aggravated by the demands imposed by industrialisation, i.e. the need to accumulate and borrow capital and to satisfy the requirements of a better-educated national population. The quoted Paris price of white sugar increased from 1,000 francs per ton in 1973 to 8,150 francs per ton by the end of 1974. It fell again to under 3,500 francs per ton by January 1975, and left many sugar dealers much richer — but some bankrupt — in the main trade centres of London, Paris, and New York.[25]

The late 1974 prices of around $US1,000 per ton persisted well into 1975, and radically changed the terms of trade for the major sugar producers in developing countries, including Jamaica. This country made heavy investments to increase plant capacity, and under a five-year programme planned to increase sugar output to more than 700,000 tons per year.[26] Other developing countries, notably Sudan with its ambitious Kenana sugar project costing more than $US600 million, rapidly began to expand production capacity. However, sugar prices fell to new historic lows by the late 1970s, reaching under $US200 per ton in late 1979 before recovering to about $US400 per ton in 1980–1. Because of the new capital-intensive plants which had been installed in Jamaica and Sudan, their unit costs in sugar production were able to fall to $US280 per ton with full capacity utilisation. However, they increased to $US450 per ton when there was only 60 per cent capacity utilisation. Hence, the effects of a decrease in sugar prices were disastrous for these countries.

Table 3.10 GDP, exports, and the role of primary product exports for selected OECD countries, 1978.

Country	*GDP ($US billions)*	*Total exports ($US billions)*	*Exports as a share of GDP (per cent)*	*Primary products as a share of exports (per cent)*
Federal Republic of Germany	754	142.1	19.1	10
France	560	76.6	13.8	24
Belgium	100	44.3	44.3	21
Italy	315	56.1	17.8	15

Sources: IBRD, *World Development Report,* 1981; and *Collections dossiers,* Brussels, CEE, various issues.

Jamaica has seen dramatic reversals in the national conception of its sugar industry. From the optimistic role forecast for sugar in the mid-1970s, Jamaican sugar production had fallen to under 250,000 tons while capacity stood at about 450,000 tons.[27] Several major factors can be identified as determinants, of which the most important was the great increase in EEC beet-sugar production from under 10 million tons per year in the late 1960s to over 15 million tons in 1981, while at the same time European sugar demand fell.[28] In addition, other producers, such as India, have recently entered the export market. India's crystal sugar output increased from 4.8 million tons in 1974 to 7.5 million tons in 1981. She therefore had to stock 4.5 million tons in 1982, making an increase of nearly 50 per cent on stocks in 1980–1.[29] The USA, the world's biggest sugar importer, rapidly introduced new, non-sugar, maize-based substitutes at well under $US200 per ton, with the result that US sugar imports have fallen by 35 per cent since 1976.

It can thus be argued that while free market speculation ushered in the brief 'sugar boom' era of the mid-1970s, which bnenefited many small, primary.producing developing countries, it also precipitated less beneficial developments. Firstly, high sugar prices, just as with cocoa, peanuts, tea, and coffee (to some extent), and also with certain hard (mineral) commodities, notably aluminium and copper, bring about specific economic and secular responses, namely:

- (i) short-term falls in demand;
- (ii) changes in elasticity function for products using high quantities of the commodity;
- (iii) new producers, particularly those using high-output capital-intensive techniques; and
- (iv) substitutes.

Secondly, no small, primary-producing developing country, whose output is small relative to world-traded quantities of a specific commodity, can invest sufficiently to protect prices of this commodity. Only organised, international action can do this, which explains the significance of the UNCTAD Common Food proposals. This common fund, conspicuous by its absence from the international scene (except for ineffective sugar agreements and, more recently, a forty-country agreement on jute),[30] would of necessity involve trade-offs between producers and consumers.

The third reason for arguing that commodity price booms are self-limiting, and can easily hurt those (the producers) who initially benefit from them, is technical. It is the problem of storage (without serious quality deterioration) at costs which the stockist — and ultimately the market — will bear. This problem is acutely important for at least three, and possibly five, of the sample countries. Soft perishable commodities, notably tea, coffee, peanuts, and sugar, are hard to store cheaply for more than a few months. With regard to tea, of which Sri Lanka was the second largest world exporter at 184 million kilograms in 1981, and Kenya the third largest at 100 million tons,[31] the potential for storage over a period of more than six months is not easy to envisage. Furthermore, Kenya, Uganda, and Rwanda, and other producers who have entered the world market only in the last ten years, are able more easily to supply the market all the year round, unlike India and Sri Lanka. Thus, the formerly strong dominance of India and Sri Lanka in world tea supply has been eroded by newer producers, able to use new concepts (including new technology and management) and to profit by different climatic conditions. It can be argued that the newer producers in the tea market are, in effect, playing a 'storage' role by their year-round production. In these circumstances it is hardly surprising that Kenya has shown little interest in the idea of a tea producers' group, or that India has expressed reserve over proposals for restricting the access of new producers to world sugar markets.

Similar arguments apply to peanuts, of which Senegal is Africa's biggest exporter with an export value of $US160.1 million out of total exports of $US512.9 million in 1978[32] An historical review of United Kingdom, French, and German policy in the West African colonies shows how important, for climatic and social reasons as well as for metropolitan market demand, was the development of peanut production in Francophone, West Africa.[33] As a direct result, many West African countries (such as Mali, Niger, and Upper Volta), are today still large producers of peanuts. They have a specialisation problem which is now more difficult to resolve because of increasing peanut output by newer, large-scale producers, notably Brazil. As a result, appeals for producer co-operation are overcome by short-term foreign exchange needs and the desire to profit by price booms, should they arrive.

3.4.3 Trade factors and the 'central hypothesis'

It will be recalled from Chapters 1 and 2 that adjustment, as variously defined, includes the following possibilities:-

(i) deflation, with slowed growth;

(ii) increased external market penetration and stronger domination of the internal market; and
(iii) funding of resource gaps through borrowing.

This subsection is concerned with the second possibility, which is also termed 'structural adjustment'[34] because it concerns long-term economic changes as well as short-term economic policy, trade, and other responses.

The reasoning behind the structural adjustment concept, so far as it relates to changes in the trade sector, is that the rises in oil prices had a sharp deflationary effect on oil-importing states (an effect often described as 'direct loss of real income'), and that therefore the response should ideally feature:

(i) increased export growth and/or
(ii) reduced import growth, and
(iii) increased home market domination.

Thus, in his study of the economic effects of oil price rises in South Asian countries, Desai[35] commented:

> The rise in oil prices and the concomitant worsening of the terms of trade transferred real income abroad from S Asia . . . The view was often expressed at the time that since these . . economies relied less on international trade and were more 'self-sufficient' than more developed economies they would be less affected by the rise in oil prices. Our calculations give no support to this opinion; [and] they show a very substantial loss of real incomes . . .
>
> These estimates of the income effect ['excess cost'] must be qualified in two respects. First, the faster the domestic output of a country is growing, the easier it should find it, *ceteris paribus*, to adjust to the loss of income . . Second, the way we have calculated the loss of income depends on the volume of imports; if a country cuts down its imports because it could no longer afford them . . it would thereby be shown to have reduced its loss of income as well.

However, it is difficult to view global changes concerning technology and new socio-political imperatives and demands, as well as economic and trade factors, in such a clear-cut way, as the direction of such reasoning is that structural adjustment modes can be reduced to just a single factor, economic growth. If, following Desai and others, the oil price rises were equivalent on each occasion to a loss of real income of, say, 1.5 to 8 or 9 per cent (depending on the country)[36] this could, in theory, be made up over three to four years by proportionate increases in GDP growth. It has already been noted (Chapter 2) that several newly industrialised countries (notably South Korea), and virtually all developed nations, took this path from 1975–6 to 1978–9.

This model of adjustment, which may be called accelerated economic growth without sacrifice, is likely to apply only to highly developed or highly dynamic economies. The delayed recovery from the second oil crisis of the OECD countries is apparently regarded as an indicator of technological weakness, requiring real sacrifice, perhaps for many years, as new infrastructures and technologies are established. Thus, in 1981, a well-known European economic commentator made this statement regarding structural transformation in the North:

> It is now more or less a consensus view among economists that the industrialised world needs to undergo a great process of structural transformation, involving massive investment in new manufacturing techniques and the development of new products. This investment is needed not just to increase output and living standards but merely to maintain them. For the explosion of energy prices, the microelectronics revolution and the rise of the newly industrialising countries is making much of the Western world's industrial capital obsolete, even while it is in perfect running order.[37]

Although the period after 1980 is outside the scope of this study, it is obvious (see Table 3.4) that only three countries in the sample —Sri Lanka, Bangladesh, and Senegal — appear to have shown increases in GDP growth rates in 1973–7 relative to the average for 1970–7. Of these, the Bangladeshi figures are open to variable interpretation (see below), while the increase in the growth rate for Sri Lanka was too small to be of any account. On the other hand, the two richest countries in the sample — Peru and Jamaica — showed a definite contractive tendency in 1973–7 relative to the average for 1970–7, with a sharp fall in their annual average GDP growth rates. This pattern of change in GDP growth rates indicates that, generally, lower-income developing countries (as in the sample) have not responded in the same way as developed or newly industrialised countries to the first oil crisis. Internal economic adjustment, through expansion, does not appear to have taken place in the sample countries, while certain countries (Peru and Jamaica) have shown a contractive response, that

Table 3.11 Export and import trends for each sample country, 1968–1979 (1975 $US throughout)

Country	*Exports ($ millions)*		*Annual average growth of exports (per cent)*		*Imports ($ millions)*		*Annual average growth of imports (per cent)*	
	1968	*1979*	*1968–79*	*1972–6*	*1968*	*1979*	*1968–79*	*1972–6*
Bangladesh	366	662	5.5	15.8	510	1,537	10.5	24.8
Sri Lanka	391	981	8.7	12.9	425	1,448	11.8	14.4
Kenya	398	1,104	9.7	19.5	397	1,658	13.9	16.8
Senegal	189	421	7.6	14.2	253	756	10.4	22.9
Peru	987	1,949*	7.1	10.3	911	2,090	7.8	23.0
Jamaica	399	769	6.1	9.7	456	1,010	7.5	11.3

* The figure for exports is for 1978; that for 1979 was greatly increased by oil export revenues, thus Peruvian oil-importing economic experience is better shown by excluding 1979 data for exports.

Sources: IBRD, *World Tables,* 1980; and IBRD, *World Development Report,* 1980, 1981.

is, deflation, with a decrease in the growth of the national economy.

In relation to external trade, the performance of the sample countries appears to support the argument that the oil crises have merely served to underline their resource gaps. As indicated in Table 3.11, *all* the sample countries showed much greater annual average import growth than export growth and only one (Kenya) showed a higher export growth rate than import growth rate in the period 1972–6, which spans the complete sequence of the first oil crisis, response, and recovery trend period. Only Kenya was able to record a current account surplus *and* a trade surplus in period (3) of the different trade-year periods outlined in Table 3.6. In addition, Kenya was the only country whose exports grew at a faster rate than imports during the same period. Nevertheless, even Kenya has ended the decade 1970–80 with a large current account deficit and, like all the other developing countries in this sample (Peru ceased to be a developing country in 1978), shows considerably higher trend import growth than export growth.

In summary, these are the findings of the analysis so far.

(i) All of the sample countries experienced negative terms of trade influences.

(ii) None of the sample countries was able to prevent rapid import growth exceeding export growth.

(iii) In this context, capture of new export markets was either impossible or extremely difficult.
(iv) Rising trade deficits absorbed capital, and thus further limited expansive adjustment by restricting rapid growth of industrial investment.
(v) Dominance of national (internal) markets was very difficult because of a weak industrial infrastructure.

3.5 Finance and debt

As with other areas, it should be noted that this one also presents serious problems regarding the accuracy and consistency of data drawn from multiple sources. For example, estimates of OPEC surpluses,[38] which have been the basis for several adjustment theories expounded by the IBRD and IMF, etc., are by no means precise. For the period 1974–80 such estimates differ by at least 25 per cent, and for 1980 the variation is in the range of 25 per cent, which is sufficient to destroy any theory on the quantitative impacts of deficits and surpluses. However, clear patterns of change in the volume and type of finance for developing countries have emerged during the study period, and in certain cases these have had precise impacts on sample countries in the group. This section reviews the major trends in the debt and finance characteristics of the sample countries and relates them to the themes of adjustment. The specific effect of direct oil account deficits on trade, and hence as a component of current account deficits and consequent borrowing requirements, is briefly reviewed here. Since the question of this effect is so basic to the underlying aim of this study, the subject is considered more deeply in Chapter 5.

3.5.1 Finance and debt — the general trends

The relationship between oil price rises and the mounting debt facing most developing countries has sometimes been described in a causal and simplistic fashion. The data shown in Table 3.12 can be used to give strong support to this causalistic approach, and hence the most common conclusions drawn from these data are that:

(i) fuel deficits (mostly oil) have increased greatly;
(ii) manufacturing deficits have not increased proportionately; and
(iii) consequently, the rising trade deficits of developing countries are solely the fault of oil import costs.

But this cannot explain the data shown in Tables 2.6 and 2.7, where the stability of fuel deficits among the various components making up trade deficits is apparent when these figures are related to the GDPs of developing countries. From these data a different rationale can be advanced, namely:

(i) trade and current account deficits of developing counties have increased greatly from 1970–80;
(ii) the relative proportion of fuel to non-fuel import (manufacturing and services) deficits has remained remarkably constant during this period; and
(iii) consequently, the fault (rising trade deficits) lies in slowed economic growth in the developing countries themselves

Table 3.12 Fuels and manufactured goods deficits, all developing countries,* selected years, 1973–1980 (1978$US throughout)

Category	*1973*	*1974*	*1975*	*1978*	*1979*	*1980*
Fuels deficit	3.88	10.6	10.0	11.6	14.8	23.3
Manufactured goods deficits	32.60	35.8	37.0	43.3	44.3	44.4
Total trade deficit	17.80	23.8	29.8	33.3	38.1	45.0

* 'Non-OPEC developing countries', i.e. includes non-OPEC oil exporters.
Source: UNIDO, *The Impact of Higher Energy Prices on the Industrialisation of Developing Countries,* Paper IS279, Vienna, UNIDO, January 1982.

These opposing rationales inevitably engender two completely different prescriptions for the adjustment of developing countries to changed external economic circumstances. Those advancing the first rationale would recommend contraction of imports (especially oil), energy conservation, and so on. Those advancing the second would argue for economic expansion, especially through the capture of export markets. Ironically, both prescriptions feature in the IBRD recommendations on policy priorities to aid adjustment in developing countries (outlined in Chapter 1).

At the individual country level, the terms of trade and export price variation problems have already been noted in Section 3.4, and these are further discussed in Chapter 4. Throughout the study period these factors, on balance, have had severe negative impacts on the economies of the sample countries, shown, for example, in the increase in public debt. In constant 1978 US dollars, the disbursed public debt of the six-country sample group increased from

Table 3.13 Current account deficit or surplus for each sample country as a percentage of GNP, selected years, 1970–1979 (current $US)

Country/factor	*1970*	*1972*	*1973*	*1974*	*1975*	*1976*	*1978*	*1979*
Bangladesh								
GNP ($US billion)	ca 3	n/a	5.89	8.23	11.48	6.72	7.55	7.62
Current account deficit ($US million)	ca 60	n/a	236	475	579	259	344	1,310
Current account deficit as % of GNP	ca 2	—	4.0	5.8	5.0	3.9	4.6	17.1
Sri Lanka								
GNP ($US billion)	1.85	1.83	1.98	2.51	2.64	2.41	2.71	3.30
Current account deficit ($US million)	57	28	21	132	106	3	58	231
Current account deficit as % of GNP	3.1	1.5	1.1	5.3	4.0	0.1	2.1	7.0
Kenya								
GNP ($US billion)	1.54	1.96	2.24	2.73	3.04	3.28	4.85	5.81
Current account deficit ($US million)	49	68	126	308	229	119	519	479
Current account deficit as % of GNP	3.2	3.5	5.6	11.3	7.5	3.6	10.7	8.2

Senegal								
GNP ($US billion)	.844	1.06	1.22	1.36	1.8	1.89	1.84	2.37
Current account deficit ($US million)	16	+10.5	101	66.5	86	92	145	437
Current account deficit as % of GNP	1.9	+1.0	8.3	4.9	4.7	4.9	7.9	18.4
Peru								
GNP ($US billion)	6.08	7.49	9.10	11.34	13.31	13.02	12.43	12.48
Current account deficit ($US million)	+202	31.5	262	725	1,541	1,193	919	+618
Peru								
Current account deficit as % of GNP	+3.3	0.5	2.9	6.4	11.6	9.1	7.4	+5.0
Jamaica								
GNP ($US billion)	1.34	2.73	1.89	2.43	2.82	2.89	2.33	2.77
Current account deficit ($US million)	153	197	248	92	283	303	142	55
Current account deficit as % of GNP	11.4	7.2	13.1	3.8	10.0	10.4	6.1	2.0

Notes: ca denotes approximate figures; n/a — no available data; + indicates current account surplus. Sri Lanka and Kenya had current account surpluses of, respectively, 5.1 and 1.4 per cent of GNP in 1977.

Sources: IBRD, *World Tables,* 1980 and IBRD, *World Development Report,* 1980, 1981, supplemented by official country sources.

about $3 billion in 1970 to over $14 billion in 1980. This outstripped both the population growth (about 30 per cent for 1970–80) and the GNP growth (about 21 per cent in real terms, all countries aggregated). The growth of public debt, in this period, accelerated rapidly from the mid-1970s for most countries, and even outstripped the problem of financing the oil imports.

But although public debt grew for all countries, it varied greatly from country to country, and by the end of the study period had become highly constrained by the relative income group of each country. Thus, the richest countries in the sample, Peru and Jamaica, borrowed most and were the only countries to show a much greater annual increase in public debt in the period (1973–6) immediately following the first oil crisis. Other countries in the sample did not record this trend: Kenya and Senegal showed their fastest growth in the period *after* 1976, whereas Sri Lanka had its fastest growth in the early 1970s. Data on Bangladesh are confused by the country's emergence from the war of independence, which created a problem for researchers of separating the economic and financial data relating to former East Pakistan from that of the new Bangladesh. However, the available data appear to indicate that Bangladesh increased its real public debt so rapidly in the period 1973–6 that it has continued to limit the country's freedom to borrow (as opposed to seeking grants, etc.) ever since. Conversely, Sri Lanka cut its debt radically after 1976, and particularly after 1978, when the country showed a 'post-oil crisis bulge' in its growth profile of interest payments. This was because changes in terms of trade and export growth resulted in a significant current account surplus in 1977. Likewise Kenya, aided by the post-oil crisis recovery of the world economy and the linked improvements in its terms of trade, also gained a current account surplus in 1977.

3.5.2 Current account deficits — and surpluses

It is in the analysis of the current account trends of the individual sample countries that the 'conventional hypothesis' encounters many problems. Above all, the data shown in Table 3.13 and Figure 3.4 do not support arguments for a strong, causal, direct link between current account deficits, growth of public debt, and the single factor of oil imports. If the analysis is confined to the period 1970–6, then the growth rate of the current account deficits of the two richest countries is large enough to swamp all other data for the sample group. But in 1979, relative to 1970, it can be seen that

Peru's current account deficit has disappeared because of oil exports. On the other hand, the current account deficits of the other countries have increased rapidly. Public debt was common, and figures indicate large debt increases for all countries during 1970–9.

Proceeding on a purely chronological basis, and considering *only* the question of current account deficits, it could be said that the first oil crisis of 1974–5 was marked in nearly all the sample countries by a rapid rise in deficits, reversed equally sharply in 1976–7. After 1979, the lower the income and the greater the primary product dependence of a country, the greater was its current account deficit, and vice versa. Senegal, Bangladesh, and Sri Lanka fall into the first category, and Peru, Jamaica, and Kenya into the second.

A closer analysis of current account deficit trends can be made by looking at changes in the growth of these deficits, as shown in Table 3.14, which highlights several trends already indicated in previous analysis. First, it should be noted that if oil price rises *were* the sole cause of developing countries' financial problems, then this

Table 3.14 Changes in current account deficit growth (annualised) for each sample country, 1970–1979

	Change in current account deficits (per cent)*			
Country	*1970–9*	*1973–6*	*1973–9*	*1976–9*
Bangladesh †	§	− 0.8	27.4	63.8
Sri Lanka †	9.5	−55.0	36.1	312.0
Kenya †	11.0	−13.7	6.5	31.7
Senegal †	28.7	−16.1	14.2	55.4
Peru ‡	4.7	46.4	16.9	− 53.0
Jamaica	−17.6	−8.8	−26.9	−42.3

* Decrease on year/period before indicated by −sign.

† These countries showed much higher current account deficit growth in 1977–80, than in 1978–80.

‡ Current account deficit growth in 1972–6 was 133 per cent per annum, due to contraction of the economy.

§ n/a — no available data.

Source: Derived from Table 3.13.

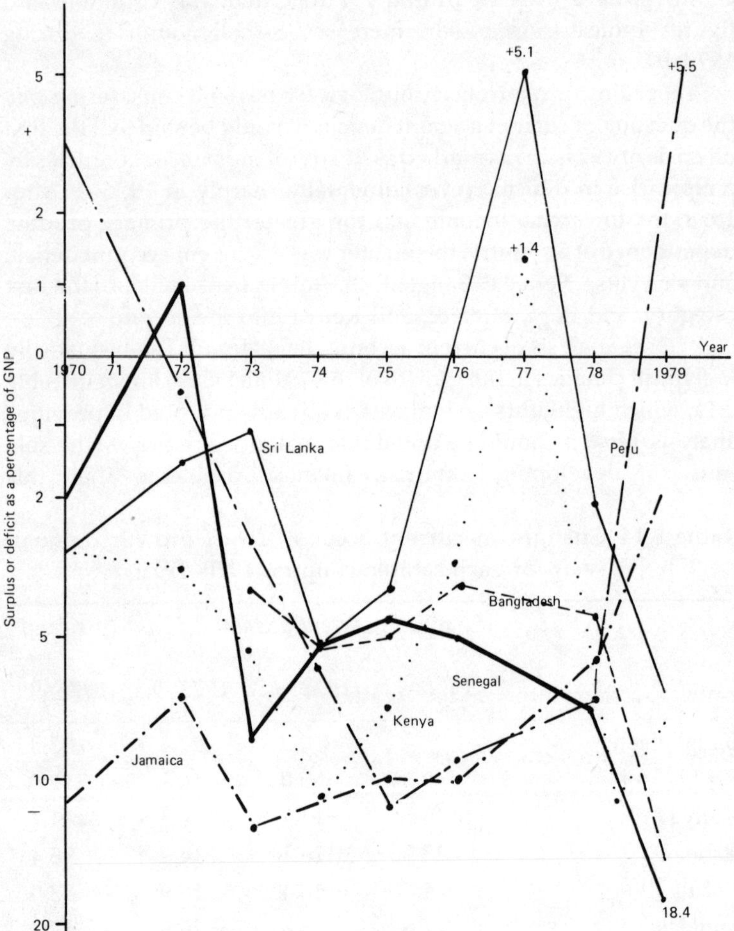

Fig. 3.4 Current account deficit or surplus for each sample country as a percentage of GNP, 1970–1979*

* *Based on data shown in Table 3.13*

analysis of a sample of developing countries' current account deficits should show at least some of the countries as experiencing rapidly growing deficits during 1973–6. Apart from Peru, which was to become an oil exporter, *not one* sample country exhibited such a pattern. Second, if Bangladesh is excluded because of its rather special character (namely, food supply problems, the war of independence, internal unrest, and climatic problems), and Sri Lanka, Kenya, and Senegal are taken as more typical of the majority of lower-income developing countries, it can be seen that these three countries showed a clear and definite pattern of financial changes, namely:

(i) very significant *decreases* in current account deficits in the period (1973–6) immediately following the first oil crisis;
(ii) large annual average growth in current account deficits (three to ten times the GNP growth rate) throughout the period 1973–80; and
(iii) very marked acceleration in current account deficits after 1976, and especially after 1977–8.

In no way does this pattern of events lend itself to the 'conventional hypothesis'. It tends, rather, to support the 'excessive debt/slow economic growth' rationale which, in turn, lends support to those policies which would accelerate developing countries' economic growth, perhaps through import substitution, or perhaps through export growth, but without such rapid increases in debt.

The performances of Peru and Jamaica show that higher-income developing countries generally exhibit less violent financial changes, probably because of the larger 'mass' of their internal economy. In addition, both Peru and Jamaica had to seek IMF support in the 1970s, and Jamaica — despite the politicised approach to 'swallowing the IMF medicine'[39] — is now a model example of IBRD/IMF 'adjustment through contraction'. The constant contraction of Jamaica's economy, which squeezed exports, eventually also squeezed the current account deficit. Whether this has left Jamaica better or worse adapted to the 1980s is another question. Peru, however, has defied economic gravity. Its current account deficit rose because military imports had increased from 10 per cent of all imports in 1976 to 23 per cent in 1977.[40] This trend was then reversed in a rapid and effortless fashion by the arrival of exportable oil surplusus, but the question of whether this leaves Peru better adjusted in the post-oil period is another matter.

3.5.3. Growth of national debts

The trends in trade and current account deficits, reviewed in the preceding sections, show a progression from bad to worse, with occasional reversals. Such reversals, whether through good crops, sudden improvements in terms of trade, better management, or cheap loans, were temporary for all the sample countries except Peru. The period after 1974 was marked by an increasing supply of private loan capital to (almost exclusively) the richer developing countries. These 'petrodollar loans' were supplied at positive real interest rates, in complete contrast to the previous trend of negative real interest on loans. Only where countries were able to acquire special facilities, notably Bangladesh (following the war of independence) and Sri Lanka (which received oil facility loans from the IMF), were the rising interest rates, and therefore total debt service increase, abated.

The debt trends during 1970–9, shown annually in current US dollars for each sample country, are set out in Table 3.15. These trends are also presented graphically to show disbursed public debt for each year (Figure 3.5) and total debt service for each year (Figure 3.6). Bangladesh presents an exceptional profile, due to the country's unusual circumstances during this period (see also Table 3.16). However, apart from Bangladesh, the progression of total public debt and intrest payments varies significantly according to each country's experience, pressures, and adjustment throughout the period. As with the progression of current account deficits, the differential rates of growth of public debt for the sample countries throughout the period 1970–9, expressed in inflation-corrected terms, provide a useful extra method for analysis, and these are shown in Table 3.16 and Figure 3.7. Apart from Bangladesh, the performance data indicate that the poorer countries in the sample experienced a decrease in real rates of borrowing in 1973–6, relative to the 1970–9 average. Of these countries, only Sri Lanka managed to hold down its percentage debt growth to single figures throughout the entire period 1970–9. Figure 3.7 clearly shows the greater borrowing propensity of the higher-income countries (and Bangladesh) in the immediate post-oil crisis period of 1973–6. Their real public debt grew at high rates *throughout* that period, but their performance after 1973–6 in income and terms of trade in the economic and trade sectors is comparable to that of the

Table 3.15 Disbursed public debt, interest payments, and total debt service for each sample country, selected years, 1970–1979 ($US millions, current for each year)

Country	*1970*	*1972*	*1973*	*1974*	*1975*	*1976*	*1977*	*1978*	*1979*
Bangladesh									
Disbursed public debt	n/a	ca 54	355	1,020	1,620	1,950	2,290	2,790	2,842
Interest payments	—	—	4.1	8	16.5	28.5	25.5	42	41
Total debt service	—	—	9.1	25	70	65	63	93	84
Sri Lanka									
Disbursed public debt	317	395	422	485	587	702	787	1,013	1,086
Interest payments	11.5	11	15.5	16.5	20.5	23	22	25	28
Total debt service	39	49.5	54.5	69	138	127	124	89	76
Kenya									
Disbursed public debt	313	373	433	498	545	672	821	953	1,427
Interest payments	11.5	14.5	16.5	18.5	20	23	31	45	60
Total debt service	27	25.5	29.5	33	34	47	54	114	104
Senegal									
Disbursed public debt	102	139	205	248	299	353	441	587	786
Interest payments	1.8	4.9	7.2	14	18.5	18	21	31	43
Total debt service	6.8	13	30	33.5	40	43	59	106	122
Peru									
Disbursed public debt	848	1,050	1,430	2,210	2,990	3,690	4,660	5,380	5,930
Interest payments	43	52	93	113	187	199	248	317	437
Total debt service	144	182	398	432	436	454	652	750	919
Jamaica								1,036	1,182
Disbursed public debt	154	210	338	512	695	875	896		
Interest payments	8.5	12	17.5	33	49	53	59.5	70	95
Total debt service	14	29	37.5	62.5	79	108	147	184	208

Notes: n/a — no available data; ca denotes approximate figures.
Sources: IBRD, *World Tables,* 1980; IBRD, *World Development Report,* 1980, 1981; and *Financial Times,* London, various issues.

Table 3.16 Growth rates of real public debt for each sample country, 1970–1979 (annualised average growth, per cent)

Country	*1970–9*	*1973–6*	*1973–9*	*1976–9*
Bangladesh	n/a*	62.9	23.4	1.9
Sri Lanka	6.2	4.5	3.2	3.9
Kenya	9.6	6.9	10.1	15.6
Senegal	16.2	11.1	13.1	17.4
Peru	15.0	26.7	14.4	5.3
Jamaica	16.2	26.8	11.2	− 0.7

* n/a — no available data.
Source: Based on data shown in Table 3.15, with inflation correction.

Thus the countries that had gained relative to the 1973–4 oil crisis were those countries whose commodity structure of exports, good crops, and favourable terms of trade lent themselves to quick increases in net trade receipts, and who were able to reduce their borrowing needs quickly. Countries in the sample that definitely experienced this sequence of events include Sri Lanka and Kenya. Senegal might have been included, but the growth of this country's debt, climatic disaster, and the rapid decrease in peanut prices all combined to prevent Senegal from financing its small GDP growth from domestic resources.

Conversely, Peru and Jamaica saw a rapid increase in import costs for oil, other primary materials, and food at a time when both countries were engaged in large, costly development programmes and projects. Both countries increased their borrowing and recorded very large annual rates of growth in real public debt in the period 1973–6. Both countries had become technically bankrupt by 1976–7 and sought emergency finance from the IMF. At this point it was inevitable that for both countries the growth rates of public debt would fall, as, indeed, they did. For Jamaica, without the benefit of oil production, and with a very heavy debt profile, the result of 'IMF medicine' was to turn the rapid annual growth in its public debt into an annual decrease.

It is appropriate at this stage to note the following general financial trends and pressures which conditioned the adjustment experience of this sample of developing countries during 1970–9, namely:

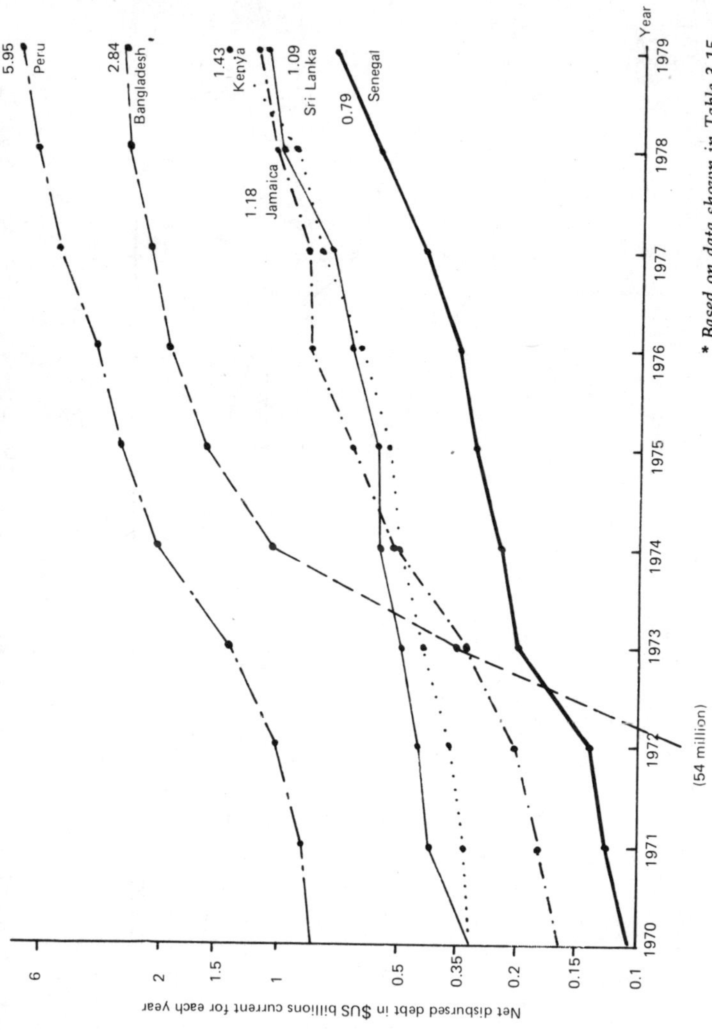

* *Based on data shown in Table 3.15*

Fig. 3.5 Net disbursed public debt for each sample country, 1970–1979*

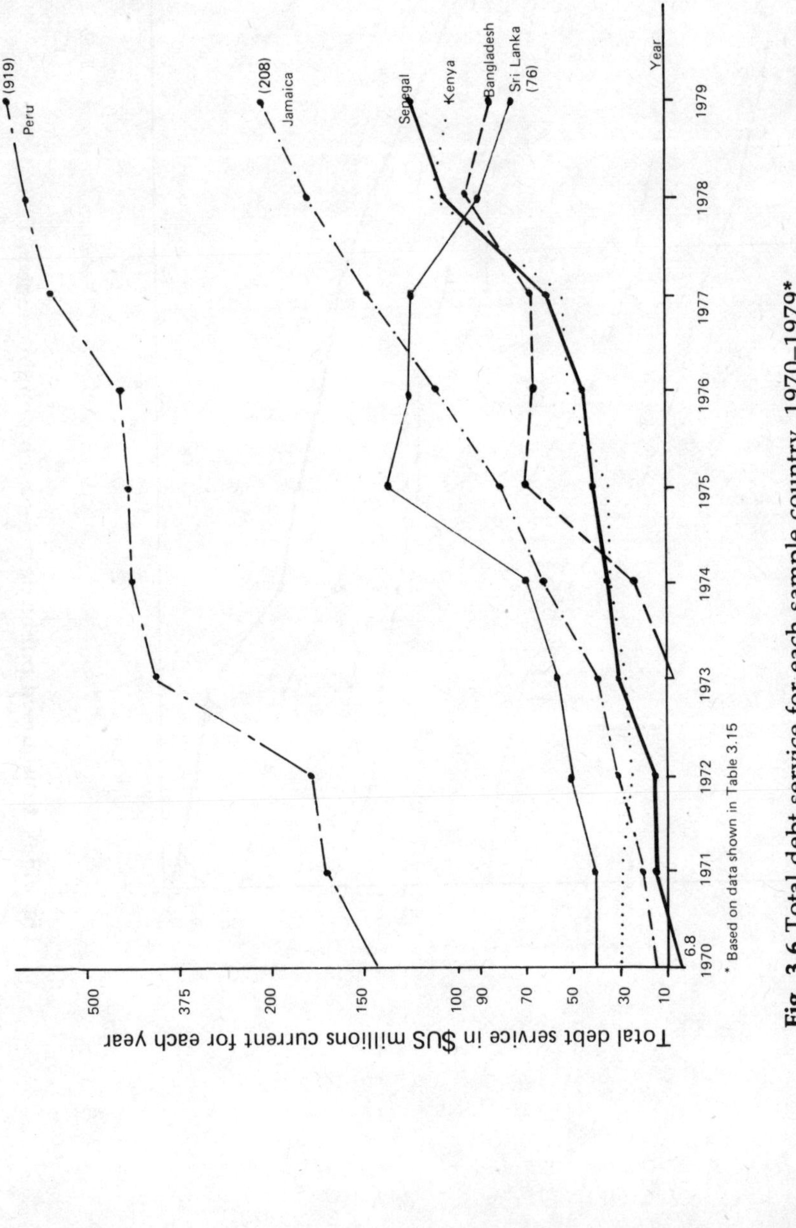

* Based on data shown in Table 3.15

Fig. 3.6 Total debt service for each sample country, 1970–1979*

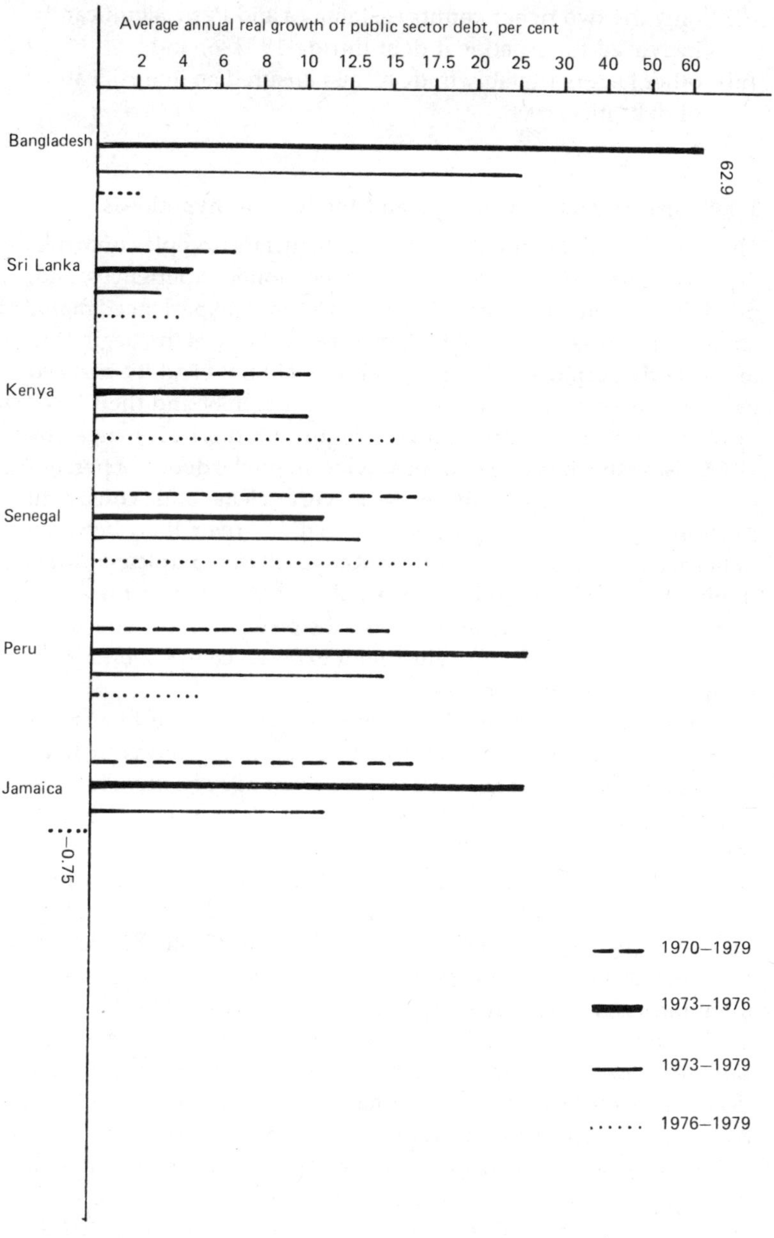

Fig. 3.7 Annual average real growth of public debt for each sample country, 1970–1979 (per cent)*

* *Based on data shown in Tables 3.15 and 3.16*

(i) all countries heavily increased their debt;
(ii) only the two richer countries, Jamaica and Peru, significantly increased their national debt during 1973–6; and
(iii) other factors (notably trade terms) ensured an intensification of debt increases.

3.5.4 Finance and debt factors and the 'central hypothesis'

The data reviewed in this section indicate that the sample countries, depending on their income, trade, and economic experiences, and, possibly, their management of debt and finance, experienced major adjustment pressures in the financial sector. Thus, at the beginning of the study period, the sample countries did not exhibit a marked correlation between the total cost of external debt and their GNP per capita. But, as is clearly shown in Figure 3.8, this had changed by 1979. Using the measure of debt service on public debt as a percentage of annual GNP, there is a very clear and consistent relationship, with high positive correlation (over 0.9), between debt service and GNP. Apart from Kenya, all the sample countries doubled or trebled their total external debt. Add to this the rising annual cost of national debt, and the trade problems, and it becomes apparent how difficult the adjustment experience has been for the sample developing countries.

It is significant that in these countries there were temporary reversals (of one to two years) of their declining terms of trade when there was an expansion of world economic activity. This describes the experience of Sri Lanka, and to a lesser degree Kenya, in the period 1976–8. For Sri Lanka, the combination of cheaper loans and greatly reduced financing requirements resulted in inflows (net of repayments) that were only 12, 38, and 17 per cent of total inflows in the years 1975–7, compared with 90, 82, and 81 per cent for Bangladesh in the same period.[41] The impact of such high repayment rates can be clearly seen in the interest payment profile of Sri Lanka, shown in Table 3.16. For Sri Lanka — but not for the other sample countries (except Jamaica, which was in continuous decline) — this improvement in national finances was aided by a contraction in imports, including oil in certain years.

It was, however, Sri Lanka, Senegal, and Jamaica which had the lowest average growth rates of GDP throughout the decade 1970–80, although Sri Lanka's low population growth rate mitigated the impact of low GDP growth rates on personal income. Senegal, on

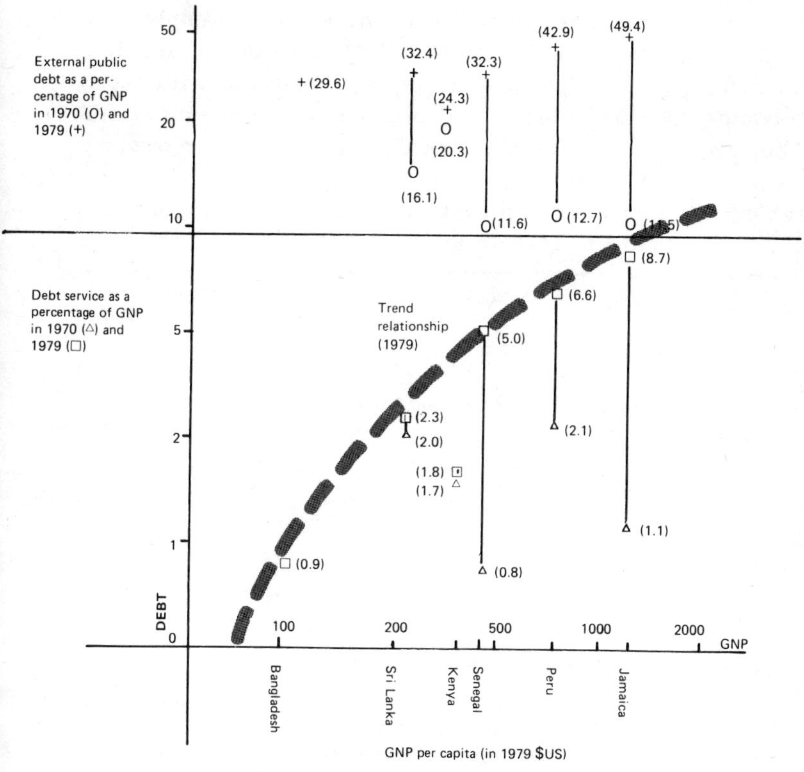

Fig. 3.8 External public debt and debt service for each sample country, 1970–1979

Sources: IBRD, *World Development Report,* 1980, 1981, and IBRD, *World Tables,* 1980.

the other hand, stood half-way between Sri Lanka and Jamaica in terms of GDP, debt growth and servicing problems, and net growth of real income per capita. Significantly, both Senegal and Jamaica experienced a bad decade (1970–80) in which there was an average annual decline in their capita GDP, and for several years both recorded falls in GDP as well. Yet both — and especially Jamaica — can be said to have shown more features of adjustment, as defined by the 'central hypothesis', than other countries in this sample. Both countries had to accept stagnation and decline ('slowed growth'), and both (particularly Jamaica) cut imports, but not in such a way as to compensate for higher import prices, poor export prices, and other problems. They also borrowed heavily to cover resource

Table 3.17 Estimates of Sri Lanka's commercial energy demand, 1970 and 1975, from two sources †

	Country paper on Sri Lanka for UNESCAP, 1979 ‡		*Asian Development Bank's Sri Lanka study, 1981 §*	
Demand sector	1970	1979	1970	1975
Hydroelectricity generation	8.27tn.BTU	12.7tn.BTU	262GWh	365GWh
In tn.BTU, converted where necessary*	8.27	12.7	3.47	4.48
Consumption of petroleum products	34.7tn.BTU	29.06tn.BTU	0.893m. tons	0.964m. tons
In tn.BTU, converted where necessary**	34.70	29.06	38.94	42.03
Consumption of coal	0.61tn.BTU	0.25tn.BTU	0.49tn.BTU	7.00ktons
In tn.BTU, converted where necessary***	0.61	0.25	0.49	0.18

*Conversion figures:** trillion BTU = 10^{12}, thus 1 GWh (1 million kWh) = 3.412×10^9 BTU, or 0.0034 trillion BTU. However, the UNESCAP source cites '1GWh = 0.01325 tnBTU', a factor presumably allowing for conversion losses.

** Petroleum products are given a value of 45GJ/ton or 43.6 million BTU/ton, i.e. 0.0436 trillion BTU/1,000 tons.

*** Coal (i.e. quality black coal) is given a value of 27GJ/ton, conversion is as for petroleum.

† The minimum variation for any one figure from these sources is 12.5 per cent, and the maximum variation is 162 per cent.

‡ Sri Lanka Electricity Board, 'Country Paper — Sri Lanka', working paper for a meeting on the use and conservation of energy, Bangkok, UNESCAP, October 1979.

§ G.B. Fernando *et al.*, *Sri Lanka Study*, Asian Development Bank, cited in CENRENIEO, *Seminar on New and Renewable Sources of Energy*, Oxford, CENRENIEO, October 1981, pp. 5–111.

gaps. Unfortunately, the external world economy, particularly after 1977–8, and much more so after 1980, did not 'adjust', and both countries now face the severest debt problems of all the sample countries.

Conversely, the two countries in the sample with the largest external debts, Bangladesh and Peru, are both exceptional cases. While Peru has — and will for many years continue to have — a large backlog of servicing costs, the 'black gold' (oil exports) will easily overcome the need for adjustment policies of the 'central hypothesis' kind. Bangladesh pays the least interest on its debt for the simple reason that it is too poor to do otherwise. For Bangladesh, the critical issue is one of basic human needs, and this features in all its development policies.

3.6 Energy

As with the data for other adjustment sectors, those relating to energy use in the sample countries throughout the study period present problems of accuracy and consistency.

3.6.1 Accuracy and consistency

This problem can easily be demonstrated by comparing, for one sample country, the available data for the *same* years from *different* sources, as in Table 3.17 on Sri Lanka. This table on commercial energy demand uses data from official country sources and from the Asian Development Bank. One of the greatest problems arising from such variability in data is that it may very easily lead to an entirely erroneous interpretation of 'trends' which, it emerges, are statistical phantoms. This problem of accuracy and consistency becomes still greater when yet more official information sources are consulted. A final example of this is given in Table 3.18, which is a summary of data claiming to show the amount of commercial energy consumed, per capita, in Sri Lanka during 1970. In this context, it should be noted that Sri Lanka has one of the more reliable data assembly systems of developing countries.

These examples of unreliable data sources reinforce the need for caution in the interpretation and use of energy data for developing normative and quantitative relationships.

3.6.2 Role of renewable/traditional sources of energy

Section 3.6.1 drew attention to major disparities in the available data on modern commercial energy use in developing countries. However, these disparities are even greater in the data on non-commercial energy use. Using various parity rates, different estimates of a country's total commercial energy use are arrived at, depending upon whether one includes or excludes household and non-commercial energy consumption. Therefore, this study uses such data with caution, and relies more on economic data for analysing adjustment.

Table 3.18 Commercial energy use, Sri Lanka, 1970, from four different sources (per capita commercial energy use in kilograms coal equivalent)

*Sri Lanka Electricity Board**	*Fernando* et al.†	*IBRD, World Development Report, 1980‡*	*IBRD, World Tables, 1980§*
129	126	95	153

Sources: *Sri Lanka Electricity Board, 'Country Paper — Sri Lanka'. † Fernando *et al.*, *Sri Lanka Study*. ‡Tables 7 and 18. §Table 9, p. 423.

3.6.3 General commercial energy trends

The main focus of this study is 'economic adjustment', especially the linkages, and strength of linkages, between economic adjustment and the energy sector. Since this concerns, above all, the modern sector, the primary focus of inquiry in the energy sector must centre on commercial energy. It is appropriate, therefore, to review the major trends in commercial energy use for the sample countries, and in this context the following factors can be observed:

(i) evidence of large changes in size, type, or use of commercial energy;
(ii) pricing changes; and
(iii) assumed, claimed, or interpreted (using relevant studies) energy-economic changes.

3.6.4 Trend changes in commercial energy use

The commercial energy consumption for each sample country is shown in Table 3.19. The data are extracted from IBRD publications and adjusted and supplemented whenever appropriate. They reflect a generally low commercial energy consumption in the sample group of countries, of which the average weighted energy consumption (including Bangladesh) was under 100 kgce per capita in

1979, or under 250 kgce per capita if Bangladesh is excluded. By comparison, the weighted average for all industrial countries in the same year was — according to the IBRD[42] — some 7,892 kgce per capita. This low commercial energy consumption in the sample countries leads to problems in weighing and analysing trends, since small quantitative annual changes in commercial energy use have large proportionate impacts on trends performance.

It is again noticeable that just one country (Peru), with very

Table 3.19 Commercial energy consumption per capita for each sample country, selected years, 1965–1979 (in kilograms coal equivalent (kgce))

Country	*1965*	*1970*	*1975*	*1977*	*1978*	*1979*
Bangladesh	n/a*	n/a	40	39	43	41
Sri Lanka	118	115	105	114	109	140
Kenya	126	135	164	141	149	180
Senegal	139	139	175	175	181	265
Peru	535	620	630	645	650	735
Jamaica	870	1,425	1,875	1,560	1,110	1,205

* n/a — no available data.

Sources: IBRD, *World Development Report,* 1980, 1981; *World Tables,* 1980; IBRD, Paper 350, August 1970; UN, *Yearbook of International trade Statistics,* various issues; and CENRENIEO, *Seminar on New and Renewable Sources of Energy.*

sizeable hydropower and petroleum resources, showed a continuous increase in energy consumption in each year of the data period for Table 3.19. Further, when corrected for population growth, this increase is shown to be rather small, of the order of 2.5 to 3.5 per cent per annum. All the other sample countries showed very low annual growth, apart from the six-year period 1970–5 (Sri Lanka excepted) and the two-year period 1978–9 (Bangladesh excepted).

Using these (Table 3.19) and other data sources, it is possible to present data relating to the period 1971–3 and compare them with the post-oil crisis performance of the sample countries. Data for the end of this period (1979–80) are, however, open to considerable uncertainty, but nevertheless are offered for review in Table 3.20. These data, when presented graphically as in Figure 3.9, allow a

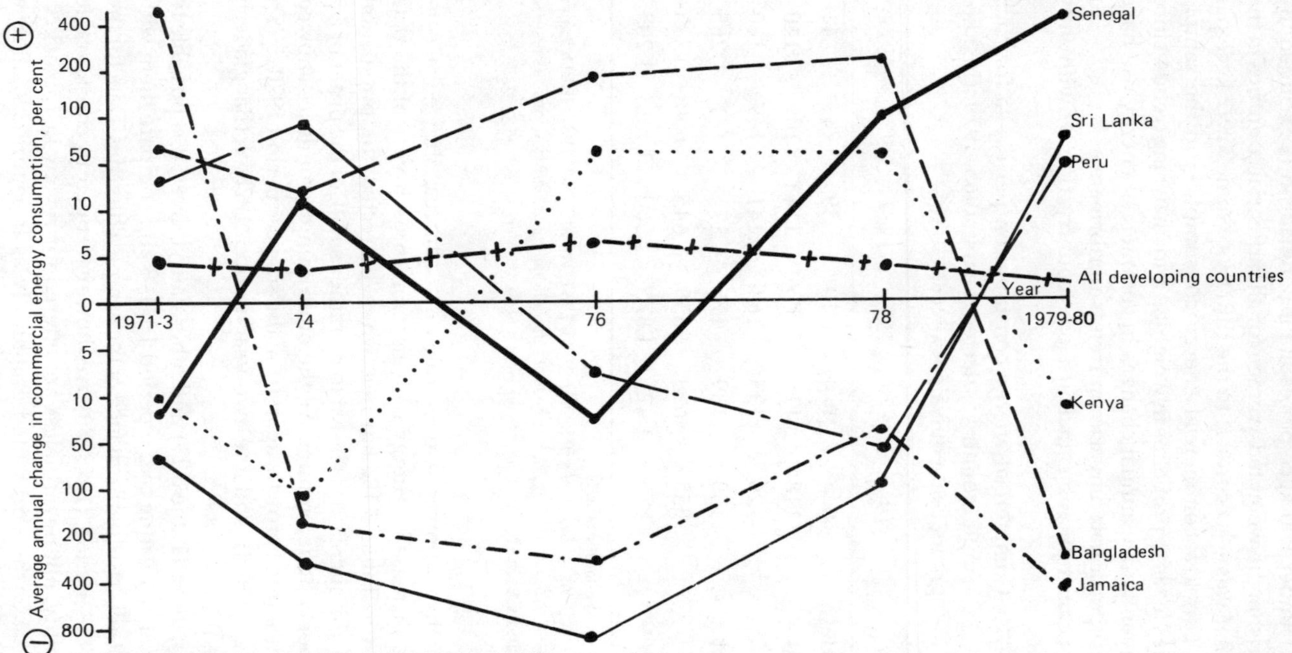

* Based on data shown in Tables 3.19 and 3.20

Fig. 3.9 Average annual change in commercial energy consumption for each sample country relative to the average for all developing countries, 1971–1980 (per cent)* comparison of the trends in the sample countries relative to that for all developing countries. (This group includes such newly industrialised countries as South Korea, and countries which showed high growth rates in energy (and therefore oil) consumption throughout the decade until 1979–80.) It is noticeable that the changes in the sample countries' commercial energy consumption, when calculated annually in relation to all developing countries, are closely related to changes in GDP, interest payments, and movements in terms of trade.

Table 3.20 Average annual change in commercial energy consumption in each sample country relative to the average for all developing countries, 1971–1980 (per cent)

Country	*1971–3*	*1974*	*1976*	*1978*	*1969–80**
All developing countries	+4.7	+3.8	+6.3	+4.1	+2.2
Bangladesh	+7.8	+12.5	+17.9	+12.7	−4.7
Variation	+66	+23	+184	+209	−310
Sri Lanka	+2.6	−8.0	−2.2	0	+3.8
Variation	−45	−321	−850	−100	+72
Kenya	+4.2	−0.6	+9.9	+6.4	+1.8
Variation	−11	−116	+57	+56	−18
Senegal	+4.0	+4.7	+4.0	+8.2	+11.1
Variation	−15	+24	−36	+100	+405
Peru	+6.4	+7.3	+5.8	+1.5	+3.3
Variation	+35	+92	−8	−63	+50
Jamaica	+20.5	−3.5	−11.3	+1.9	−6.8
Variation	+440	−192	−285	−45	−410

* Most recent estimate.

Sources: As for Table 3.19, and C. Wolf *et al.*, 'Estimating energy demand in oil-importing developing countries', *Energy Journal*, 2/**4**, October 1981; and B.J. Choe, *Energy Demand in Developing Countries*, Washington DC, IBRD, 1981.

With regard to changes in GDP (see Table 3.4), it is significant that those sample countries which showed relatively high rates of GDP growth during 1973–5 (Kenya and Senegal), also showed the highest growth in commercial energy consumption relative to all developing countries in the same period. Countries which experienced little GDP growth (notably Sri Lanka) or stagnation (Jamaica), recorded the largest falls in commercial energy consumption relative to all developing countries.

With regard to interest payments (see Table 3.15), those countries which showed the highest growth in annual interest payments — Peru, Jamaica, Bangladesh, and Senegal — in the period 1972–5, also (apart from Senegal), recorded the sharpest falls in commercial energy consumption relative to all developing countries in the same period. However, Senegal and Peru, which were gaining on terms of trade movements relative to 1970–3, did show a major contractive response in the *energy* sector in 1974–6, when the *combination* of decreased or stagnant GDP growth, increasing current account deficits (see Figure 3.4), and sharply raised interest payments resulted in very sharp reductions in their ability to pay for imports. Again, by the end of the study period Kenya and Bangladesh were recording sharp rises in interest payments abroad, and sharp falls in commercial energy consumption relative to all developing countries.

The general performance of Jamaica tends to support the inferred strong linkage between the energy sector and the three economic factors identified earlier. As Jamaica has the most energy-intensive economy of all the countries in the sample, it could be expected that economic adjustment *primarily* related to energy price changes would be demonstrated by this country. Unfortunately for this analysis, Jamaica emerges — somewhat like Peru, Senegal, and Bangladesh — as a 'special case', due to the fact that the country recorded essentially zero growth, and a small decrease in GNP, during the whole study period. Since its aluminium and sugar industries account for over 60 per cent of GNP, and aluminium is an energy-intensive material (257 MJ/kg finished metal, and around 20 MJ/kg alumina ore),[43] the interplay of just two factors is sufficient to explain Jamaica's pattern of adjustment. These factors are the world prices for sugar and alumina (and their effects on Jamaica's terms of trade), and the cost of energy imports, which led to national debt problems.

Thus, economic stagnation, declining terms of trade, and rising debt have led to a consistent reduction in Jamaica's energy consumption since 1972, the last year in which there was any real growth of GDP. It is therefore of great significance that Sri Lanka's energy consumption declined significantly between 1974–6, especially in comparison with the consumption rates of other developing countries. In this period a stagnant GDP, combined with sharply rising interest payments, had a strong impact on Sri Lanka's energy use. However, in the preceding period (1972–4), when Sri Lanka's GDP had increased significantly, and exports had increased by 70 per cent in current rupees, the difference in commercial energy consumption between Sri Lanka and all developing countries was much smaller.[44] The fact that Sri Lanka's commercial energy consumption did not grow even more significantly in this period can be explained by unfavourable terms of trade movements — while the volume of output in Sri Lankan industry from 1972–4 was constant, export volumes in 1974 were some 13 per cent *below* those for 1972.[45]

The terms of trade, therefore, appear to complete the group of deterministic economic factors which influenced the levels of commercial energy consumption for the sample countries during the study period. Kenya, which experienced a decline in terms of trade from 1970–1 to 1973–4, showed relatively low (1971–3) and very low (1974) growth in commercial energy consumption during this period. However, the sharp recovery in Kenya's terms of trade from 1975–6, and the moderate growth of the country's debt (despite quite fast-growing interest payments), completely reversed this pattern. Thus, from 1976–8 Kenya showed a noticeable growth in commercial energy consumption well above the average for all developing countries.

Jamaica showed gains in terms of trade in 1975–7 (i.e. during the sugar boom and when aluminium prices were high). This trend was accompanied by a radical fall in commercial energy consumption below the average for all developing countries. It is possible that the time lag between the reversals of terms of trade, trade deficits, increased current account deficits, higher borrowing, and increases in interest payments caused the country to record an *increase* in commercial energy consumption in 1978, whereas Jamaica is shown to have quite significantly *decreased* its total use of petroleum in 1978 for most sectors, as compared to 1977, and to have shown an increase in commercial energy consumption in 1978 relative to 1977 of less than 0.5 per cent.[46] Thus, the reversal in Jamaica's terms of trade in the period 1975–7 correlates quite well with a reversal in the declining trend of Jamaica's energy consumption.

In the case of Sri Lanka, there is a close correlation between changes in terms of trade and changes in commercial energy consumption. Sri Lanka experienced a relative gain in terms of trade at the beginning (1970–3) and the end (1978–80) of the study period. Equally, the negative spread of the country's growth rates in commercial energy consumption, compared with the average for all developing countries, was much smaller in 1971–3 than in 1976, and by 1970–80 Sri Lanka showed growth rates in commercial energy consumption *above* the overall developing-country average.

3.6.5 Energy-economic intensities

It is notable that with regard to energy intensities, the measure of GDP or GNP output per unit kilogram of coal equivalent (kgce) commercial energy input (1 kgce = 28.2 MJ) is often treated as highly deterministic, and as showing very tight elasticity functions. Estimates of the elasticity functions of commercial energy for developing countries vary considerably according to the country's income group, and over short-term (generally one to three years) and long-term (over one to three years) time periods. Nevertheless, some clear trends are apparent, and it is found that this sample of developing countries tends to conform to these trends. The most significant trend is that of a gradual increase of energy intensities in the economy with industrialisation. This trend can be explained by the factors accompanying industrialisation, such as the decreased role of agriculture, urbanisation, the growth of physical and social infrastructure, and so on. In addition, some economists claim that the elasticity functions of commercial energy have fixed income elasticities and low price elasticities for developing countries, and that these tend to increase with every successive decrease in income. Others claim that the fixed income elasticities and low price elasticities are almost uniform for most developing countries. The performance of European Community motorists, when faced with the first oil crisis, bore very little relation to supposedly 'fixed' price elasticity, and this suggests that large factor price changes in the economy do no easily lead to large changes in long-term consumption when any alternative solution is available.

For the purpose of this study, major attention has been given to the role of energy intensities in the development of the sample countries throughout the study period. The base data (see Table 3.21) use the measure of energy intensities per unit GNP, expressed in constant 1978 US dollars. While GDP measures would be preferable, as GNP can vary significantly for external factors (such as large, externally funded projects),. the problem of converting GDP to constant dollar prices poses many problems of its own. GNP figures (often converted to US dollars) are used in official data, and data sources such as the IBRD frequently use the measure

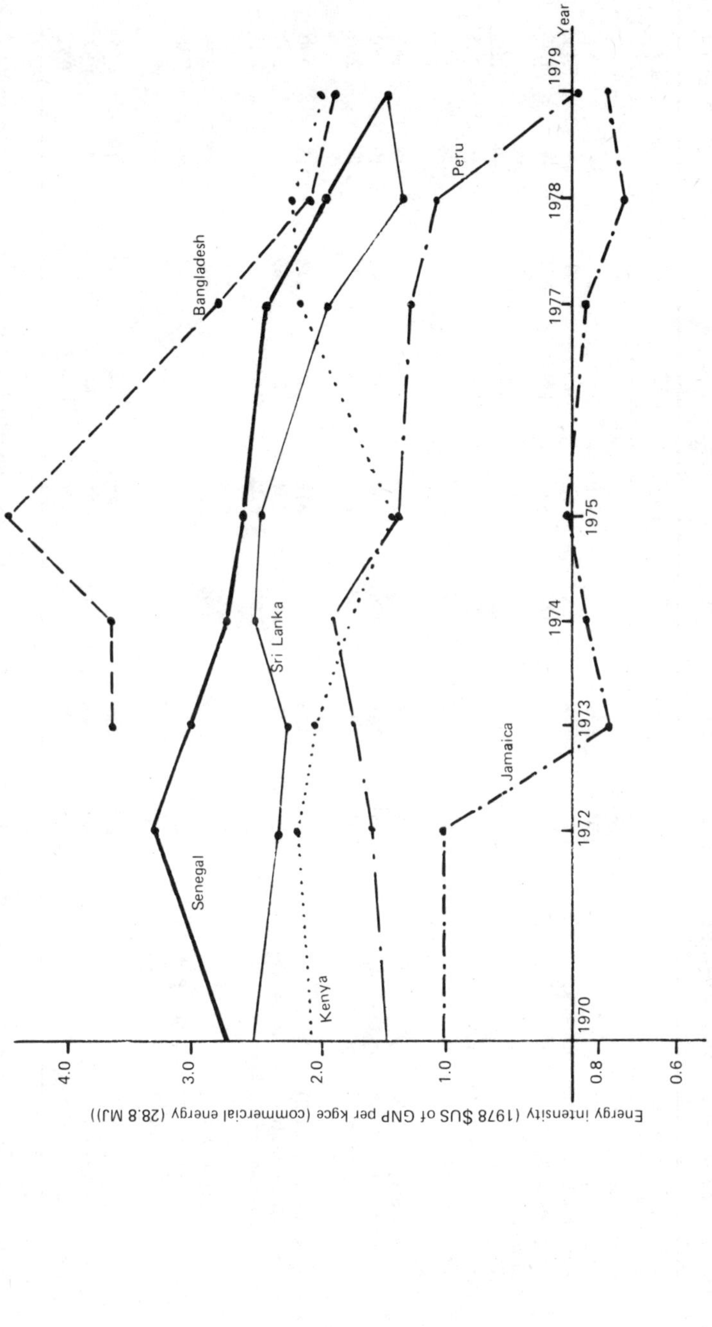
Energy intensity (1978 $US of GNP per kgce (commercial energy (28.8 MJ))
4.0
3.0
2.0
1.0
0.8
0.6
Year
1970
1972
1973
1974
1975
1977
1978
1979
Bangladesh
Senegal
Sri Lanka
Kenya
Peru
Jamaica

Fig. 3.10 Energy intensities for each sample country, 1970–1979*

* *Based on data shown in Tables 3.19 and 3.21*

Table 3.21 Energy intensities per constant 1978 $US of GNP in each sample country, selected years, 1970–1979

Factor and country	*1970*	*1972*	*1973*	*1974*	*1975*	*1977*	*1978*	*1979*
Bangladesh								
GNP per capita ($US)	n/a*	n/a	137	150	180	100	89	80
Commercial energy per capita (kgce)	n/a	n/a	38	41	40	39	43	43
Energy intensity ($US/kgce)	—	—	3.63	3.65	4.50	2.78	2.08	1.90
Sri Lanka								
GNP per capita ($US)	291	270	264	277	252	212	189	206
Commercial energy per capita (kgce)	115	116	118	110	102	114	138	205
Energy intensity ($US/kgce)	2.53	2.32	2.23	2.52	2.47	1.87	1.37	1.47
Kenya								
GNP per capita ($US)	275	308	316	286	250	307	329	362
Commercial energy per capita (kgce)	135	141	156	165	174	141	149	180
Energy intensity ($US/kgce)	2.04	2.18	2.03	1.74	1.42	2.17	2.20	2.01
Senegal								
GNP per capita ($US)	386	435	451	412	460	410	345	390
Commercial energy per capita (kgce)	139	131	149	151	175	169	181	260
Energy intensity ($US/kgce)	2.78	3.32	3.03	2.73	2.61	2.43	1.91	1.47
Peru								
GNP per capita ($US)	890	990	1,090	1,150	895	890	740	675
Commercial energy per capita (kgce)	620	630	635	638	640	645	650	735
Energy intensity ($US/kgce)	1.44	1.57	1.70	1.81	1.40	1.35	1.14	0.92
Jamaica								
GNP per capita ($US0	1,490	2,002	1,760	1,870	1,880	1,560	1,115	1,205
Commercial energy per capita (kgce)	1,425	1,960	2,240	2,075	1,805	1,660	1,690	1,575
Energy intensity ($US/kgce)	1.05	1.02	0.76	0.90	1.04	0.93	0.66	0.76

* n/a — no available data.

Sources: As for Table 3.19, and Jamaican Petroleum Corporation, *National Energy Outlook*, Kingston, JPC, October 1981; IBRD, *Commodity Trade and Price Trends*, Washington DC, IBRD, August 1981.

of GNP in US dollars.

The data problems noted earlier must again be emphasised, since there are very great variations in data from different sources. Thus, by way of another example, the Jamaican Petroleum Corporation lists Jamaica's total oil consumption in 1978 as 16.510 million barrels of fuel oil equivalent and notes that, in that year, 98.8 per cent of the country's commercial energy was petroleum-derived.[47] Using the stated conversion factor for fuel oil (1 barrel = 6 million BTU), this gives a commercial energy consumption per capita of 1,758 kgce. The IBRD *World Development Report* of 1980 lists 1,823 kgce per capita for Jamaica in 1978, a 4 per cent difference. For 1979, the 1981 *World Development Report* lists a 1,390 kgce per capita commercial energy consumption for Jamaica, while for the same year the Jamaican Petroleum Corporation lists a practically unchanged 16.30 million barrels of fuel oil equivalent,[48] giving 1,730 kgce per capita, a 25 per cent variation with the IBRD figures. Other sources, such as the EEC data bank,[49] provide yet other figures, which easily maintain variations ranging, typically, from plus to minus 25 per cent.

Among the data presented in Table 3.21, those for Bangladesh and Peru are probably the least reliable, although data on Peru improved considerably after the 1977–8 'co-operative assessment' programmes of the US Department of Energy and the Egyptian and Peruvian governments. The data from Table 3.21 are also presented graphically in Figure 3.10, which allows certain broad trends, and links with previous adjustment sector analysis, to be identified. Notably, the general, slow increase of energy intensities in the economies of the sample countries stands out. Without exception, all countries were obtaining fewer US dollars of constant GNP for each kilogram of coal equivalent energy used in 1979, relative to 1970.

Within this general pattern, other factors relating to economic change can be identified. Increases of energy intensities have not been progressive and incremental, but fluid, changing quite rapidly at certain periods. It can be seen that Kenya greatly *decreased* its energy intensities between 1975 and 1977, and Senegal showed a *decreasing* trend in 1970–2, while Peru has shown a sharp increase in energy intensities since 1977. The energy intensities of Jamaica showed a large increase from 1970–3, followed by a period of stabilisation, while those of Sri Lanka showed most *decrease* in the period 1973–5. These performances show that predictions based on the numerical relationships of fixed income elasticities or price elasticities are highly aggregated, and inapplicable to individual countries.

This evidence leads to certain conclusions (presented in Section 3.6.7) about adjustment theory. In particular, it should be noted that there is very little evidence of *abrupt* changes in energy intensities after the first oil crisis, except in Jamaica, the most energy- and petroleum-intensive economy of the sample. The best correlations with changes in energy intensities — as with adjustment in general — relate to changes in trade, terms of trade, and current account trends, as can be seen by a comparison of Figure 3.10 with Figures 3.2, 3.3, and 3.4.

3.6.6 Energy pricing

Among the orthodoxies concerning energy-economic policy responses to higher oil prices, that of 'progressive taxation' can be singled out as easily the most popular. As the IBRD stated in its *World Development Report* of 1980:

> Although higher base prices for energy have encouraged more economical use, their effects have been muted because taxes have not risen as much . . . The sharp rise in oil prices in 1973–4 reduced the relative importance of taxation in every kind of petroleum product; little has been done since to restore it. In the early and mid '70s, the reluctance of governments to add to inflation often took precedence over conserving energy by raising its price.[50]

As can be seen from partial price data (shown in Table 3.22) relating only to the years 1973 and 1977 for four countries of this sample, the general tax declined quite significantly from 1973–7. However, in relation to GNP per capita, or to world oil prices, these petroleum prices at the retail level were very high. These data, though very partial, do indicate that after the first oil crisis only Jamaica and Kenya maintained a progessive tax policy on car transport fuel, while Sri Lanka introduced a heavy tax on industrial (residual) fuel oil. On this evidence, using a conventional OECD analytic frame of reference, only Jamaica might be said to have made a positive response. Yet the briefest comparison of these pricing data (Table 3.22) with available personal income figures for the economies of OECD countries, as against the economies of developing countries, shows how enormous are these prices. Further, the industrial use of commercial energy in developing countries (such as those in the sample) is generally much *higher* than in OECD Northern countries if one considers the prooprtion of all commercial energy going to primary and secondary industry, relative to that used for commercial and residential purposes. In 1978, about 38 per cent of the average commercial energy use of all developing countries was in mining, manufacturing, and agriculture, as against 26 per cent in the same year for the same three sectors in developed countries.[51] The average for developing countries conceals great variations, as

Table 3.22 Petroleum product prices for four of the sample countries, 1973 and 1977 (constant 1973 $US throughout, US cents/US gallon)

Country and year	*Regular gasoline*	*Kerosene*	*Auto-engine distillate*	*Residual fuel oil*
Jamaica				
1973 retail	37.6	14.7	16	10.8
1973 tax	13.6	0	0	0
1977 retail	117.8	21.9	18.7	12.6
1977 tax	72.7	0	0	0
Peru				
1973 retail	21	4	15	11.2
1973 tax	8	0.2	0	0
1977 retail	61.1	7.9	13.8	7.9
1977 tax	20.3	0.4	0.6	0.5
Kenya				
1973 retail	59	33.3	28.5	19.2
1973 tax	31.3	7.2	n/a*	n/a
1977 retail	82.1	45.3	58.5	n/a
1977 tax	36.1	3.9	15.1	n/a
Sri Lanka				
1973 retail	71.7	17.5	n/a	11.2
1973 tax	31	5	n/a	0
1977 retail	96.5	26.3	39.6	33.0
1977 tax	17.3	2.1	3.2	2.3

* n/a — no available data.

Source: Derived from IBRD, *Energy Options and Policy Issues for Developing Countries*, Washington DC, August 1979, Tables VI–IX, X, with inflation correction (price deflator).

certain high-income, newly industrialising countries — notably Taiwan and Singapore — have little, or zero, mining and export-oriented agriculture, while by contrast Jamaica uses about 50 per cent of all its commercial energy just in its alumina and bauxite industry. In 1976, Bangladesh used about 20 per cent of its total petroleum import content in the form of fertilisers.[52]

These factor considerations are perhaps not well appreciated in industrialised countries, where the combined services and residential use of commercial energy can account for over 60 per cent of total commercial energy use. Thus in developing countries price elasticity of demand (that is, reductions of use per unit increase in price) is low — typically, —0.08 to —0.1 for developing countries compared to —0.3 to —0.4 for OECD countries.[53] Faced with this inelastic demand, energy policy makers in developing countries cannot freely apply swingeing taxes in the hope that the oil problem will 'go away'.

3.6.7 The energy sector and the 'central hypothesis'

The data which have been presented in Section 3.6 confirm, on balance, the trend of conclusions developed in previous sections. That is to say, only the higher-income developing countries in the sample (in effect Jamaica, since Peru has become an oil exporter) have shown a major contractive response in their commercial energy use during the study period. Although Sri Lanka did show quite large reductions in per capita commercial energy use from 1973–5, these reductions can be linked to changes in trade and finance. Few other sample countries showed large 'breaks' in their pattern of commercial energy use, and since all the countries in this sample (except Peru) obtain 75 per cent or more of their commercial energy from petroleum imports, their ability to pay for their increasing energy requirements can thus be identified as a key factor in this analysis. Several countries in this sample have developed major long-term energy programmes oriented to diversification and development of indigenous sources. In the shorter term, and certainly during the study period, it is very clear that large-order economic and financial factors were, and will continue to be, more important in establishing energy demand patterns in these countries than an abstract consideration of the 'energy crisis' rationale, which advocates quick cutbacks in commercial energy use.

If the data shown in Figures 3.9 and 3.10 are related to those shown in Figures 3.2, 3.3, and 3.4, then it is apparent that there is a close relationship between *financial and economic constraints* and the commercial energy consumption profile of a country. During the study period, increasing trade and current account deficits, linked to falling terms of trade, tended to depress commercial energy demand in the sample countries. Conversely, a relaxation of these financial and economic constraints quickly re-established commercial energy demand. The fact that the economies of all the sample countries (except, perhaps, those of Bangladesh and Senegal) are, in many ways, advancing their development in infrastructure and services helps to explain the general trend towards increasing energy intensity (see Figure 3.10).

As in previous sections, on this evidence it is possible to argue either for or against the 'central hypothesis'. Depending on the weight attached to the GNP income group of the sample country, it can be argued (following the case of Jamaica) that economic contraction and reduction of commercial energy use, used to reverse heavy current account deficits, are sucessful adjustment strategies. On the other hand, Sri Lanka and Kenya have shown how very quickly commercial energy growth re-establishes itself when better trade terms, declining trade and current account deficits, and invisible inflows (workers' remittances in the case of Sri Lanka and investment in the case of Kenya) are in the ascendant.

3.7 Special factors

The sample countries, like many other developing and developed countries, experienced an eventful decade in 1970–80. In some ways, the incidence of 'special factors' in the development of the sample countries was very high, which poses formidable problems in generalising from conclusions based on their adjustment experiences to those of other developing countries. In order that the extent and importance of these special factors in the sample countries may be appreciated, they are divided into political and social, climatic, and economic categories.

3.7.1 Political and social factors

Bangladesh has been severely affected by political and social constraints. Following many years of Bangladeshi–Punjabi animosity, and probably triggered off by the 1969–70 cyclones which killed about 400,000 people, the war of independence broke out in 1971. With India's aid, the (West) Pakistani forces were defeated, but not before extensive damage to the economic and social infrastructure had taken place.

Several billion US dollars, in the form of aid and relief funds, came to Bangaldesh in the three years after formal independence, but this has in no way relieved the critical poverty of this country. From 1975 (when Mujibur Rahman was assasinated) to 1979 there was a military dictatorship, and since then there has been a very troubled 'quasi-democracy'. These and other factors have left Bangladesh extremely aid-dependent, and with major infrastructural problems in all sectors.

Both Sri Lanka and Jamaica experienced major political and social stresses throughout the study period. For Sri Lanka these took place in the period 1972–7, when the Bandaranaike Government was challenged first by external (non-parliamentary) groups, and then by opposing parliamentary forces. From 1977 in Sri Lanka, and 1980 in Jamaica, more conservative, 'market conscious' governments took power, dedicated to reducing taxes and government spending. Peru also experienced a succession of poitical upheavals, though these were not excessive by Latin American standards. They encompassed the political unrest following a major earthquake in 1970, and the 1975 riots which led to the fall of the government. Kenya, after the death of Kenyatta in 1979, altered its political orientation and offered increasing facilities for non-African business and trade.

3.7.2 Climatic and environmental factors

Bangladesh, together with Senegal and to a lesser extent Peru, suffered from climatic and environmental problems during the study period. Bangladesh in particular has experienced many severe climatic problems throughout the decade. Except for 1975, when there were unusually good harvests, the country has faced recurrent, often large, floods and cyclones. While the worst were in 1969–70, many others during the decade have caused great damage, notably loss of crops.

In terms of the number of people affected by climatic and environmental crises in any of the sample countries, it is Senegal that stands out. After 1973, and at least until 1976, catastrophic drought in West Africa (and in all Sahel countries to varying extents) reversed in a few years the progress of decades. Gradual improvements in agricultural output in the Sahel countries were replaced by sharp falls in output, increased import needs, and vast human problems. While climatic change or cyclicality is undoubtedly involved, the role of increasing population pressure on wood and other biomass energy resources is certainly also part of the cause. The results, however, are clear: from being a food exporter (rather than only a peanut exporter) Senegal became, by 1973, a large food importer. From 1973–7 the country received food aid of at least 150,000 tons of cereals alone, but this met only part of its needs. It is possible that Senegal may need ten years or more to rebuild livestock herds, re-establish farming, and resettle displaced people, and this is only possible if there is no deterioration in the climatic conditions.

Climatic and environmental problems, linked to overfishing, help to explain the virtual collapse of Peru's fishing industry in the years 1973–6. Until then, fishmeal production and royalties from foreign-owned fishing operations had assured substantial export earnings.

3.7.3 Economic factors

As noted in previous sections, all the sample countries were differently affected by sudden reversals in the export prices of primary products, and certain countries were worse affected than others. Such were Sri Lanka, which suffered a 70 per cent worsening in terms of trade from 1971–4; Bangladesh, which experienced a continuous worsening in terms of trade; and Jamaica, which even by the end of the decade had not recovered from the 1971–3 reversal of terms of trade, unlike several other countries.

On the other hand, many countries in the sample received 'windfall gains' from sudden spurts in the export prices for their products, and in this category can be cited Sri Lanka (1974–8), Kenya (1976–8), and Senegal (1970–2). The most exceptional example, however, is clearly Peru, which from being a small and declining oil producer became — through heavy investment — a significant oil exporter in 1978. It is also possible to cite, although it has a much smaller potential, the increasing gas production of Bangladesh.

3.7.4 Impacts of special factors

These factors are special because they have had notable, though imprecise, impacts on the adjustment experiences and responses of the sample countries in the decade 1970–80. Some stand out, and are summarised as follows for each sample country.

Bangladesh This country experienced large aid and relief fund inflows, especially in the period 1972–5; continuing inflows of cheap loans; and, after 1975, specific aid from the Gulf states.

Sri Lanka In the period 1972–5 the country received major OECD support linked to both political and economic problems. Changing terms of trade and the market-oriented governments after 1978 appear to indicate that export growth and industrialisation will be advanced as this country's basic economic policy.

Kenya After gaining significantly on terms of trade (after 1976 in particular), the country now faces major political, social, and financial problems. In the early years of the decade, Kenya's central role in the now dissolved East African Community brought it major invisible earnings.

Senegal After gaining on terms of trade early in the decade, the Sahel disaster has routed the country's economic prospects. Declines in peanut prices, fast-rising debt, and very weak industrial development complete the structural checks on any adjustment bar a resort to increasingly difficult borrowing.

Peru Throughout the greater part of the decade Peru suffered heavily from international economic and internal political problems. Only the rapid increase in oil production has (dramatically) reversed a basic economic structure poorly adapted to any adjustment except increased borrowing.

Jamaica This country has suffered the same problem as Peru, but does so from a resources base which excludes any hope of oil production. The country's dependence on energy-intensive primary product exports ensures that the terms of trade, and perhaps industrialisation, provide the best opportunities for future adjustment. In debt terms, this country has perhaps the worst problem of all the sample countries.

Notes

1. In the period 1973–8 some 72 per cent of all developing countries' oil imports went to the following countries: Brazil, South Korea, India, Turkey, Taiwan, Cuba, Thailand, and the Philippines. See M. Desai, 'Effects of the rise in oil prices on South Asian countries, 1972–78', *ILO Review*, 120/2, March–April 1981.

2. H. Chenery *et al.*, *Patterns of Development,* Oxford, Oxford University Press, 1975.
3. Ibid.
4. Marga Institute, 'Technological and employment implications of higher oil prices: Sri Lanka', WEPR Working Paper 44, Geneva, ILO-BIT, 1979
5. IBRD, *World Development Report,* New York, Oxford University Press, 1980, p. 90.
6. L. Schipper *et al., Measuring Energy Conservation in Kenya,* Paper 12741, Cal., Lawrence Berkeley Laboratory, 1981.
7. IBRD, *World Tables,* Baltimore, Johns Hopkins University Press, 1980, Series III, p. 416.
9. ILO/DANIDA, *Manpower Assessments and Planning in Asia,* Geneva, ILO, 1978.
9. L. de Silva, *Unemployment and Economic Development,* Colombo, Ministry of Planning and Economic Affairs, 1976.
10. Marga Institute, op. cit.
11. Chenery *et al.,* op. cit.
12. N. Girvan, *Development Dialogue,* **2**, 1980.
13. W. Robichek, 'The IMF's experience in facilitating adjustment in the Commonwealth Caribbean', seminar on adjustment policies, London, Commonwealth Institute, 27–30 April 1982.
14. Asian Development Bank, *Rural Asia: Challenge and Opportunity,* Manila, ADB, 1977.
15. P. Svunkel, 'Development and environment in Latin America', *Cepal Review,* **12**, 1980.
16. See, for example, L. Rodin and N. Bazilevich, *Primary Productivity of the Main World Ecosystems,* The Hague, First International Congress of Ecology, 1974.
17. Data obtained from S.R. Eyre, *The Real Wealth of Nations,* London, Arnold, 1978.
18. See I. Kravis *et. al., A System of International Comparisons of GNP and Purchasing Power,* Washington DC, IBRD, Johns Hopkins University Press, 1975.
19. IBRD, *World Tables,* 1980, 1981.
20. IBRD, *World Development Report,* 1980, 1981.
21. E.g. IMF, *International Financial Statistics,* Washington DC, IMF, various issues.
22. A report on the UNCTAD jute pact in *Le Monde,* Paris, 7 October 1982.
23. P.L. Eckbo, 'Perspectives on North Sea oil', *International Review of Energy,* October 1980.
24. S. Al-Shaikhly, in *8th Roundtable Conference on Energy and Economic Development,* Zagreb, Institute for Developing Countries, October 1980.

25. See, for example, K. Lamalle, *Le Roi du sucre,* Paris, J-C. Lattes, 1981.
26. *Financial Times,* London, 10 April 1981.
27. *Financial Times,* London, 18 February 1981.
28. 'Dépression persistante sur les matières premières', *Le Monde,* Paris, 3 August 1982.
29. C. Prasad and K. Bhat, 'Prospects for ethanol fuel in India', in M. Chatterji, *Energy and Environment in Developing Countries,* Chichester, John Wiley, 1981.
30. *Le Monde,* Paris, 7 October 1982.
31. *Financial Times,* London, 2 September 1981.
32. From the data bank on ACP states, EEC Directorate-General for Development, Brussels.
33. See, for example, S. Amin, *Neocolonialism in West Africa,* Harmondsworth, Penguin African Library, 1971.
34. E.g. B. Balassa, IBRD Working Paper 464, Washington DC, IBRD, 1981.
35. Desai, op. cit.
36. For Bangladesh, for example, the loss of income is put at 9 per cent —see R. Islam, 'Some economic implications of higher oil prices: Bangladesh', ILO Working Paper 52, Geneva, WEPR, November 1979.
37. A. Kaletsky, 'Recovery delayed', *Financial Times,* London, 8 June 1981.
38. R. Sobhan, 'Mechanisms for chanelling OPEC surpluses', *Third World Quarterly,* 2/**4**, October 1980.
39. N. Girvan, 'Swallowing the IMF Medicine in the 1970s', *Development Dialogue,* **2**, 1980.
40. Comonwealth Institute, *The World Economic Crisis,* Economic Paper 13, London, Commonwealth Secretariat, September 1980, p. 215.
41. Desai, op. cit.
42. IBRD, *World Development Report,* 1981, p. 147.
43. Battelle Columbus Laboratories, 'Energy use patterns in metallurgical and mineral processing;, Report PB245759, BCL, 1975.
44. Marga Institute, op. cit.
45. Desai, op. cit.
46. See, for example, IIASA, *Energy in a Finite World, Paths to a Sustainable Future,* Vol. 1, Ballinger, Energy System Programme Group, IIASA, 1981.
47. Jamaican Petroleum Corporation, *National Energy Outlook,* Kingston, JPC, October 1981, pp. 181–6.
48. Ibid.
49. Statistical Office of the EC (SOEC), EEC, Luxembourg.
50. IBRD, *World Development Report,* 1980, p. 15.

51. Commonwealth Institute, op. cit.
52. Islam, op. cit.
53. C. Wolf *et al.*, 'Estimating energy demand in oil-importing developing countries', *Energy Journal,* 2/**4**, October 1981.

4 FINANCIAL ADJUSTMENT IN THE SAMPLE COUNTRIES

4.1 Introduction

Throughout the study period, and particularly after the first oil crisis, there was some attempt to focus on oil financing problems, but the funds allocated to finance the oil-induced balance of payments deficits were much too small for their needs. Further, these funds were soon withdrawn to be replaced by, essentially, two major financing systems. The first was a greatly expanded level of private bank and other commercial loans to developing countries, and the second was through debt refinancing and resources to conditional IMF loans.

Four countries in this sample are very heavily indebted and only one of these has any hope of painlessly restoring its 'soverignty' over its own financial management. The probably exaggerated role, under IMF/IBRD auspices, of deflationary policies as the major adjustment response makes the possibility of rapid progress in poor developing countries even more remote. Financial constraints appear to offer little, other than short-term contractionary checks on rising oil spending, and through limiting costly investment in power, fuel, and industrial development, they may prolong the adjustment period unnecessarily.

4.1.1 Financial responses to the oil crisis

As energy — derived to a great extent from oil — has become a basic factor in production, development prospects for any developing country can be said, following Chenery *et al.*,[1] to be based on the following three factors: population size, resource endowment, and access to capital. These three basic factors can help us to decide the outer constraints on any development plan. As Chenery *et al.* state:

> From an empirical standpoint it is very difficult to separate the effects of development policies from the underlying structural [factors conditioning them] . . . In extreme cases — such as the existence of rich mineral resources — the structure dictates the policy . . . Virtually all countries with rich mineral deposits have

used them as a basis for exports, which consequently affects their patterns of trade, production and imports . . . Even in this case, however, the [developing country] policymaker must decide how long to pursue a policy of extreme specialisation and when to shift to other patterns of trade, production and exports.[2]

In varying measure, all the sample countries studied here are facing exactly this problem, especially if the category 'rich mineral resources' is extended to include non-mineral, agricultural soft-commodity export crops, such as coffee, tea, sugar, vegetable oils, hides, peanuts, spices, and other crops exported by this sample of countries. On the other hand, Bangladesh and Sri Lanka are undoubtedly facing the problem of surplus labour, with its pressure towards policies favouring the rapid growth of labour-intensive, import-saving industry.

For all the sample countries, however, the problem of access to capital depends to a large, and always important extent on the establishment of development programmes. Thus, the availability and real cost of finance for development is critical in deciding how, and at what rate, programmes for investment (future consumption) and for current standards of living (current consumption) can be improved. At this point it is important to note that major theories have been developed[3] to define the role played by higher oil prices in the major changes that took place throughout the 1970s in the international monetary and financial systems.

The 'deflationist' school of thought argues that the oil price rises were responsible for the rapid transfer of very large sums of foreign exchange from oil-importing to oil-exporting countries, forcing the developing countries to adopt deflationary policies because of a sudden worsening of their current account deficits. In many cases, the exponents of this argument go on to claim that inflation was 'detonated' by the first oil crisis, if not by the second. This, of course, raises immediate problems of a theoretical nature, most notably the question of how a deflationary event can have such important inflationary consequences. Furthermore, the facts simply do not support the argument that oil imports brought about inflation. From 1974–6, the average rate of increase in all consumer prices in the twenty-country UNESCAP group of developing countries (including Sri Lanka and Bangladesh) decreased from 27.9 to 9.6 per cent per annum, and eventually to 1.0 per cent per annum.[4] If large oil import price rises had 'fuelled inflation' it was certainly a rather short-lived inflation. Similarly, the role of higher oil import prices was not noticeable in the twenty-three Latin American countries (including Jamaica and Peru) in the period 1979–80. In 1979 the all-country consumer price index increased by 53.8 per cent, and by an almost unchanged 53.6 per cent in 1980.[5]

While it is impossible to argue that oil import price rises set off a chain reaction of inflation, with the probable need at some stage to introduce deflationary policies, it is certainly true that oil price rises make short-run budgetary problems more severe and create a demand for new loans. The scale of these increases in borrowing varies for each country according to several factors, notably its GNP income group, the dynamism of its economy, and the cost and availability of extra financial resources.

4.2 Finance gaps and resources

As already noted in Chapters 2 and 3, the *external* economic environment — overwhelmingly the OECD countries in this case — is critical in deciding the growth and development prospects of any free-enterprise developing country. As will be seen in Chapter 5, the financial requirements for industrialisation sufficient to attain the goals of the 1974 Lima Plan are very large. The IBRD forecasts for the growth possibilities of developing countries in the period 1980–90 call for significant growths in real GDP. The financial resources required to achieve these levels of growth are shown in Table 4.1.

A number of central points emerge from these projections, relating to the role and importance of oil imports in the mix of financial elements. Table 4.1 is based on a real rate of increase in oil prices of 3 per cent per annum, and assumes that there is no significant increase in indigenous oil production or other forms of commercial energy (i.e. a nearly constant oil import elasticity function is implicit). The scenario depicted in Table 4.1 shows some disparity with the projections of the capital investment needs of certain development sectors, as advanced by the IBRD. Taking just the electrical power sector, the IBRD estimate given in 1980 for the investment needs of all developing countries in the period 1981–90[6] amount to about $US14 billion at 1980 prices or about $US300 billion at 1977 prices, using a price deflator developed for this study. Yet the data shown in Table 4.1 indicate *total* investment needs for all sectors of developing countries of about $US1,400

Table 4.1 The investment needs of developing countries 1980–1990 using IBRD 1979 'low case', or 1980 'high case', assumptions* (1977 $US throughout)

Bloc and factor	*1980*	*1990*
Total developing country oil imports ($ billions)	58	198
Of which middle-income developing countries ($ billions)	54.4	148
Current account deficits		
Poorer developing countries ($ billions)	7	12
Middle-income developing countries ($ billions)	36	27
Capital inflow needs		
Poorer developing countries ($ billions)	9	33
Middle-income developing countries ($ billions)	47	95
Total GNP		
Poorer developing countries ($ billions)	195	300
Middle-income developing countries ($ billions)	795	1,375

* The terms 'low case' and 'high case' follow IBRD terms used for projections in IBRD, *World Development Report,* New York, Oxford University Press, 1979, 1980, 1981.

Source: UNIDO, *The Impact of Higher Energy Prices on the Industrialisation of Developing Countries,* Paper IS279, Vienna, UNIDO, January 1982.

billion at 1977 prices. While the electrical power investment projections incorporate quite high-growth assumptions and, especially, also include the ambitious power plans of the oil exporters, the developing countries' component is still at least 70 per cent, or about $US210 billion at 1977 prices.

If it is assumed (see Chapter 6) that energy investments outside the electricity sector must at least equal those inside it, the the 1980–90 investment needs for the total energy sector in developing countries amount to around $US460 billion at 1977 prices,[7] or more than 33 per cent of total needs. This is a very high percentage, even after a decade of 'energy crisis' mentality in development and financial institutions, both in the North and the South. To appreciate just how extreme these figures are, these data can be compared with those for the United Kingdom under the assumptions, for the United Kingdom, of (*a*) high GDP growth (over 2 per cent per annum for forty years) with high energy intensities (no decline from the 1975–80 averages), and (*b*) the rapid development of synthetic natural gas (from coal or oil) and the rapid expansion of nuclear power. Notably, the data used for the United Kingdom in Table 4.2 are based on continuing energy independence. This is an issue which figures prominently in most developing countries' programmes on energy investment.

Table 4.2 UK energy investment scenario (constant 1976 £UK throughout)

Investment need energy sector	*Period*		*Capital investment as a percentage of GDP*	
	1990-2000	*2000-2010*	*1990-2000*	*2000-2010*
Coal (£ billions)	2.99–3.7	3.1–3.5	0.17–0.2	0.14–0.15
Oil (£ billions)	9.3–11.7	2.4–4.6	0.53–0.67	0.1–0.2
Gas (£ billions)	2.5–2.7	0.8–2.3	0.14–0.16	0.03–0.1
Nuclear (£ billions)	11.5–13	27.5–30	0.7–0.74	1.2–1.3
All conversion technologies* (£ billions)	2.4–4.9	4.2–4.5	0.14–0.3	0.2–0.2
All distribution technologies* (£ billions)	7.6–7.8	8.6–14	0.42–0.44	0.4–0.59

* Conversion technologies are those for producing synthetic natural gas; distribution technologies include all electrical power distribution, pipelines, and district heating.

Source: G. Michael Turner, Y-ARD Consultants, 'Capital costs of energy supplies', paper presented at SSRC seminar on alternative energy resources, London, 27 February 1979.

Table 4.2 depicts the investment requirements of the energy sector in the United Kingdom. It is based on the following assumptions:

(i) no effective conservation;
(ii) increased energy efficiency in industry; and
(iii) energy-limiting factors, such as environmental concerns.

Therefore, total capital investment needs for internal power and energy systems are well below 3 per cent of GDP, and require only an additional 2.2 per cent of GDP under the highest level of oil imports. This analysis draws attention not only to the small role of energy investment in a developed economy (such as that of the United Kingdom), but also to the low capital assumptions made by the IBRD about developing countries' investment needs *outside* the energy sector. Notably, the argument is either that much larger growth in real GNP is required, or that large energy investments relative to GNP are not attractive because the role of oil imports in GNP will continue to grow (see Table 4.1) despite these heavy investments in the energy sector.

It is here that the concept of finance gaps is most appropriately located. Thus, it can be argued, the weight attached to short-term growth-oriented adjustment, as against long-term structural adjustment, is critical in deciding how to evaluate the importance of borrowing for different purposes. In the analysis of adjustment *vis-à-vis* the oil crises the following choice is evident: lending to cover short-term balance of payments deficits, or lending for structural adjustment.

From the evidence of the IBRD and IMF analysis of adjustment (see Chapters 1 and 2) it appears that lending for structural adjustment has been given top priority in the international financial institutions, while short-term financing needs have been largely met by an increase in private capital flows. However, this is by no means the most satisfactory balance between long-term, low-interest loans (such as those from the international financial institutions) and short-term, high-interest private loans. On a purely analytical basis, it can be argued that the latter (private loans) should go to longer-term development projects offering secure and continued returns on investment, while short-term adjustment problems (caused by a sudden upsurge in factor prices or costs of an essential import, or by any *unforeseen* event) should be financed by the development of lower-cost, perhaps automatic, loans or grants. However, this study approaches the question of 'finance gaps' in the context of the existing pattern of financing, since the latter, ideal, pattern has not become established. All the evidence indicates that high-cost private loans have financed short-term gaps, of which the impact on trade deficits of oil price icreases is a notable example. This then leaves a 'gap' which it is only possible to 'fill' by the application of one of two starkly opposing measures (*a*) very fast growth of exports, but not the consequent terms of trade reversals; or (*b*) continuous contraction of the economy. It is not an intended irony to remark that only the richer developing countries can realistically contemplate the use of either of these measures in response to finance gaps or (to a lesser extent) adjustment pressures.

4.3 Institutional responses

Since the time of the first oil crisis there has been an acknowledgement of the need to help adjustment, both in the short term and the longer term. Indeed, the IBRD now offers texts which describe models for predicting the increase in borrowing needs (in terms of elasticity of propensity to borrow for (*a*) each 1 per cent increase in borrowing needs, and (*b*) each 1 per cent increase in oil import prices)[8] relative to changes in GDP income group and other factors. These models present certain 'ideal cases' which bear — frankly — little relation to the actual experience of many developing countries. This is because, as the IBRD report itself states: 'The estimated magnitudes of optimal borrowing are quite insensitive to the cost of borrowing, i.e. the demand [for loans] is very interest inelastic. If interest rates were to be zero instead of 10%, the estimated optimal borrowing would only be 6% larger.'[9]

The report goes on to point out that the really crucial factor is the quantity of private, and therefore high-cost, loan funds available to developing countries to cover short-term finance gaps, as against the availability of those from official sources at much lower interest rates. Unfortunately, the strongest trend, at least during 1975–8, was for a rapid increase in private loans to developing countries and a stagnation in the level of Official Development Assistance and low-cost official loans. A major study by UNCTAD/UNDP on the adjustment experience of thirteen developing countries (including Jamaica, Peru, and Sri Lanka) during the period 1970–6 concluded that general deflationary policies (which is often, in fact, the real meaning of 'structural adjustment') only have a role to play in a situation where excess demand for imports of all kinds can be demonstrated. Where this is not the case, as in most of the poorer developing countries (and in many middle-income developing countries also), deflationary policies, featuring the role of *private* loans in short-term adjustment, are very likely to do more harm than good.[10] This is particularly so because the investment share of GDP can be easily squeezed (unlike consumption), making *real* long-term adjustment through development even more difficult.

Here it is important to note that only Sri Lanka, in this sample of developing countries, has shown significant investment growth from the 1950–70 income-group average. All the other countries, particularly Peru and Jamaica, were in the 'low investment' category typical of many primary-producing developing countries in the 1970s. For such countries the obvious need is for flexible, rapid, unconditional, and low-cost loans for short-term adjustment. In recognition of this need (but not, unfortunately, in its satisfaction) the IMF established certain special adjustment funds after the first oil crisis. These included the compensatory financing facility, the extended facility, and the oil facility.[11] Of these, the oil facility can easily be singled out as the fund which had the greatest potential, but which in reality proved to be of very little significance. The various IMF facilities, and their size and usage, are shown in Table 4.3.

The inadequacy of these resources may be judged by comparing the sums lent by the IMF under various special programmes (most

Table 4.3 IMF facility drawings by all developing countries, 1974–1979

	*Drawings (+) and repayments (−) (in SDR billions)**					
Title of facility	*1974*	*1975*	*1976*	*1977*	*1978*	*1979*
Gross drawings	1.701	1.959	2.749	0.725	1.029	1.390
Repayments	0.412	0.429	0.769	0.984	1.722	1.138
Net resources	1.289	1.530	1.980	−0.259	−0.693	0.252
Oil facility	0.765	1.274	0.500	−0.178	−0.613	−0.398
Compensatory facility	0.075	0.096	1.141	−0.023	0.067	0.005
Extended facility	—	0.008	0.090	0.170	0.072	0.132
Credit tranche	0.264	0.082	0.057	−0.050	−0.163	0.244

* SDR = special drawing rights, varying from 1 SDR = $US1.2025 in 1974 to 1 SDR = $US1.252 in 1979.

Source: Commonwealth Institute, *The World Economic Crisis*, Economic Paper 13, London, Commonwealth Secretariat, September 1980, p. 57.

of which are reflected in Table 4.3) with the trends of developing countries' trade, fuels, and current account deficits. Several criticisms can be made of the oil facility, the first of which is that of its total resource availability (about $US1 billion), some 61 per cent was taken by three OECD countries (Italy, the United Kingdom, and France) and Israel,[12] none of which can be termed 'developing' in the normal sense of the word. Secondly, the facility was phased out just at the time when oil import costs were becoming a real problem for three of the sample countries, as is shown in Table 4.4. At this time terms of trade were changing rapidly, and as a consequence the developing countries were unable to adjust by broadening their export base in such a short time.

Table 4.4 The ratio of petroleum imports to total export receipts for three of the sample countries, 1973–1980 (per cent)

	Ratio of petroleum imports to total export receipts							
Country	*1973*	*1974*	*1975*	*1976*	*1977*	*1978*	*1979*	*1980*
Bangladesh	6.8	20.7	25.1	30.1	45.5	32.3	22.5	ca 30
Sri Lanka	11.2	25.8	21.9	24.1	20.9	18.2	26.6	ca 27
Jamaica	17.14	27.1	24.87	32.48	40.61	32.37	41.1	48.1

Note: ca denotes approximate figures.

Sources: Bangladesh and Sri Lanka — UNESCAP, 'Development strategies in the 1980s in the ESCAP region', *ad hoc* inter-governmental meeting on strategies for the 1980s, Bangkok, UNESCAP, August 1979; and Jamaica — Jamaican Petroleum Corporation, *National Energy Outlook*, Kingston, JPC, October 1981.

As Table 4.4 clearly shows, the ratio of oil import costs relative to export earnings was considerably higher during 1976–9 than it was during the disbursement phase of the IMF oil facility in 1974–6, which was discontinued at exactly the time (1976 onwards) when terms of trade were unstable and beginning to have a severe effect on many of the developing countries. This pattern is clearly shown by comparing Table 4.4 with the trends in trade, current account deficits, and terms of trade analysed in Chapters 2 and 3. But, as elsewhere, it should be noted that the available data are far from reliable. With regard to the data shown in Table 4.4 the Commonwealth Institute,[13] for example, gives equivalent ratios for Bangladesh and Jamaica as, respectively, 25.7 and 18.2 per cent for 1973, and 30.4 and 31.9 per cent for 1977, variations that easily span the 'plus or minus 25 per cent' range previously noted as typical.

Thirdly, as well as the inadequacies of distribution and timing, there is also the question of the magnitude of IMF facilities. A comparison of the IMF special adjustment funds (Table 4.3) with the scale of the current account or trade deficits of all developing countries shows that their fuels deficits increased (exactly as indicated for the three sample countries in Table 4.4) quite significantly from 1974–7, which was the adjustment phase after the first oil crisis. Yet by 1977 the IMF special facilities were already 'in the red', that is, they were taking more out of developing countries than they were putting resources into them. At this point, it was inevitable that those countries able to do so (perhaps only the higher-income developing countries) turned to the market in order to gain short-term adjustment funds. As already remarked, from the beginning of the decade until 1975, and especially from 1975–8, private bank and institutional loans to developing countries grew very rapidly. The change in the attitudes of lenders to borrowing is probably one of the most important (and perhaps durable) causes of the current deflationary trends which have prolonged the contraction phase of world economic adjustment after the second oil crisis. As *Le Monde* commented:

> The disinflation currently taking place poses redoubtable problems for wage-price bargaining in the [French] economy. For thirty years, real economic growth permitted large growths of salaries but this was silently financed, in part, by the constant impoverishment of all lenders. Today these lenders are, conversely, in the ascendant due to the appearance of positive interest rates, while borrowers – notably entrepreneurs — must support charges that, in the absence of moratoria, look to push many of them into bankruptcy.[14]

Exactly the same rationale applies to the debt problems of developing countries. In a review of LIBOR (London Interbank Borrowing Rate) spreads on loans from the private market (for example Euromarket loans) to a group of middle-income developing countries in 1978, it was found that (except for the oil-exporting states in the sample) the minimum spread was 1.0 per cent above LIBOR, while many countries, such as Peru, Jamaica, Kenya, Thailand, and Turkey, were paying 1.25 to 1.50 per cent above

LIBOR rates.[15] Naturally, the lenders of such profitable funds were prepared to accord quite lengthy maturities of between ten to fifteen years.

However, this longer-term, high-cost lending, to cover what at best were short-run adjustment problems (trade and current account deficits), contained the seeds of its own downfall. Falling rates of economic growth, sudden swings in terms of trade, and wildly ambitious development programmes, combined with growing debt problems, threw many developing countries into bankruptcy. For the poorer developing countries the problems were in some ways worse: lacking the capacity to borrow large funds, they now saw their only 'lifeline' — trade growths and terms of trade improvements — drifting away in a rapidly worsening world recession.

Table 4.5 Jamaica's oil imports and current account deficits, 1973–1980 (current $Jam. millions, (−) denotes deficit)

Factor	*1973*	*1974*	*1975*	*1976*	*1977*	*1978*	*1979*	*1980*
Oil imports	71.5	194.7	202.9	200.4	219.6	215.6	331.2	451.1
Current account deficit	164.3	151.8	257.0	275.2	61.9	86.7	142.6	204.2
Capital inflows, all sources	124.7	221.1	189.9	41.5	51.7	9.8	−0.4	162.5
Non-external debt	0.15	0.234	0.353	0.422	0.452	1.14	1.291	1.545

Source: Jamaican Petroleum Corporation, *National Energy Outlook.*

An example of how these problems have affected the most petroleum-intensive developing countries in the sample is seen in Jamaica's recourse to first private, then IMF loan funds during the 1970s. The effective collapse of foreign capital inflows, including loans and investment from private sources, between the end of 1975 and the end of 1979 is remarkable (see Table 4.5). The Jamaican interpretation of these trends has already been cited.[16]

However, the IMF has shown every sign of regarding Jamaica's economic management as suspect. One IMF official remarked:

> The large government deficits (funding a social welfare programme) crowded out the private sector from access to domestic bank credit, raised dramatically Jamaica's external public debt and weakened critically the balance of payments... [In the years after 1973] Jamaica's official international reserves were

> drawn down rapidly until they were depleted by early 1976 . . . since the terms of trade losses were not self-correcting they called for adjustment measures . . . . Jamaica's balance of payments was also affected adversely by a number of endogenous factors, among them excessive government spending; a drying up of private capital inflows and a flight of domestic capital . . . .; and production bottlenecks caused *inter alia* by forced changes in the ownership of certain key sectors, by excessive government regulations, by emigration of many Jamaicans with . . . scarce skills.[17]

It is ironic that the Capital Surplus Oil Exporters, having forced changes in the ownership of oil production systems, and having embarked on liberal-spending social welfare programmes, are regarded by the IMF and other institutions as a source of adjustment funds to accomplish exactly the reverse form of development in other developing countries. Jamaica was forced to go to the IMF, but because of the collapse in international investor confidence — for whatever reason — the IMF funds (first obtained in late 1973) were exhausted by early 1976.

After 1976, private investment in Jamaica collapsed and, as a high-income developing country, it was unable to obtain soft IMF loans under the other facilities. The Jamaican economy contracted virtually throughout the 1970s, and oil imports in quantity terms stabilised at around 16 million barrels per annum. However, the decisive factor was almost unquestionably the sudden slump in sugar prices and the continuing downward drift of aluminium prices (apart from short upturns, such as that between 1974–6).[18] It has already been noted how sharply trade terms declined for Jamaica from 1971–2 onwards and this, rather than the unequal struggles of the Manley governments against 'IMF medicine', dealt the Jamaican economy a heavy blow. Thus by 1979 the economy had drifted into annual decreases in rates of GDP ranging as high as 5 to 7 per cent, and the IMF policy (accepted in practice by the Jamaica People's National Party) of constant mini-devaluations led to real social hardship, including very high inflation rates.

For the People's National Party, however, the slow reduction in the current account deficit, brought about by constant economic contraction, came much too late. The social conflicts aggravated by the 'IMF medicine' led to the success of the Labour Party in the October 1980 elections on a platform of financial orthodoxy that received rapid approval from the IMF. It is notable that this new government may in fact succeed in effecting a tight money and export-oriented growth programme based on attracting foreign capital. This is because the Jamaican economy is now, to use an IBRD term, 'lean and competitive', after six to seven years of continual decline. In addition, of course, a new government espousing policies identical to those of the first two years of the Reagan Administration is regarded as a very solid bet in US private investment circles.

Because of the unhappy, and almost certainly wasteful and unnecessary experience of Jamaica's adjustment through contraction, with its inevitable social and political consequences, the IMF has reviewed the size, duration, and conditionality of adjustment funding.[19] Possibly as a direct result of the Jamaican–IMF conflict, there has been a large increase in loan funds available to developing countries with adjustment problems. The amounts theoretically available increased from 225 to 480 per cent of country quota between 1973 and the end of 1980, thus raising the total finance available from 6.7 billion SDR in 1973 to 13 billion SDR at the end of 1980.[20] In addition, from early 1977 the IMF, using proceeds from the sales of IMF gold reserves pledged by member countries (a process that has been vigorously criticised as accelerating monetary instability),[21] established the Trust Fund to provide almost unconditional funds to developing countries, particularly the poorer developing countries. On this basis the IMF can argue that — in theory — the complete current account deficit of all developing countries in 1979 (but not 1980) could have been met through IMF resources. But given the experience of Jamaica, Peru, and many other developing countries that have had to adopt quite rigid deflationary policies (quickly abandoned by Peru with the onrush of oil), it is not altogether surprising to observe how small the actual

Table 4.6 Role of IMF loans in the current account financing of all oil-importing developing countries, 1973–1979 (SDR billions)

Factor	*1973*	*1974*	*1975*	*1976*	*1977*	*1978*	*1979*
Current account deficit	9.4	28.5	31.5	22.4	18.5	25.5	32.3
Deficit or surplus after capital flows	0.5	+1.4	10.5	13.3	+1.5	4.7	6.6
Net IMF loans	−0.1	1.3	1.5	2.0	−0.3	−0.7	0.3

Source: Commonwealth Institute, *The World Economic Crisis.*

role of the IMF has been. The data in Table 4.6 are derived directly from IMF data, and by presenting them *after* taking into account capital flows, including high-cost private credits, the small size of IMF adjustment-funding is made to appear rather more significant than it really is. In fact, in relation to the gross current account deficits of developing countries actual IMF loans never reached more than 10 per cent of needs.

The general conclusions from this section tend towards the rationale that stabilised terms of trade for primary commodity exports, in an expanding world economy, offer more practical means for real adjustment in developing countries than a more narrow policy of import contraction. The latter, as Desai has noted, can easily lead to a contraction of capital goods imports as well. In his analysis of adjustment experience in Bangladesh, Sri Lanka, Pakistan, and India during 1972–8,[22] and in his detailed analysis of the Indian experience,[23] Desai develops the argument that the oil crisis of 1973–4 led to an 'excess cost', or deflationary income loss, of about 1.5 per cent for India and (following the analysis of R. Islam)[24] as much as 13 per cent for Bangladesh. However, Desai's analysis can be construed either as supporting IBRD adjustment concepts, or as highlighting the finance gaps needed to assure rapid growth, thus easing adjustment problems. As Desai notes:

> These estimates of the income effect ['excess cost'] must be qualified in two respects. First, the faster the domestic output of a country is growing, the easier it should find it, *ceteris paribus*, to adjust to the loss of income . . . Second, the way we have calculated the loss of income depends on the volume of imports; if a country cuts down its imports because it could no longer afford them at worsened terms of trade, it would thereby be shown to have reduced its loss of income as well. This is the case with Sri Lanka . . . The effects on components of income are less easy to trace, but there is at least one strong indicator that investment was curbed more severely than consumption: the share of machinery in the imports of Sri Lanka, India and Pakistan fell.[25]

As Desai, Islam, and others remark, the role of the terms of trade has been more than passingly important in exacerbating (in the case of Bangladesh), or in very rapidly reversing, a deficit situation in trade and the current account.

4.4 Finance and the 'central hypothesis'

It should be noted that there is no real dispute over the need for developing countries to borrow additional funds in order to cover short-term balance of payments problems. However, there is real dispute as to the length, conditionality, size, and use of such funds in achieving adjustment. It is critical to determine the naure of the financial problem if one is making a decision on according funds to a developing country. Essentially, IMF loans only relate to 'last resort' sources of short-term funding. To date, they have been overwhelmingly associated, by necessity, with the deployment of sharply deflationary economic and financial policies. In the case of Jamaica it can be argued that they have 'worked', since Jamaica is climbing, slowly, out of its economic morass. But the social cost has been high, and the economic cost can be gauged by estimating the amount of additional GDP that would have been generated if its growth had (at the very least) kept pace with Jamaica's population growth (about 1.6 per cent per annum). This gives a rough figure of $Jam. 1.25–1.6 billion, a figure very close to the entire national debt of Jamaica. Undoubtedly Peru would also have experienced Jamaican IMF-style adjustments, were it not for oil.

All of the sample countries have radically increased their debt, with the exception of Sri Lanka, which nevertheless raised its national debt twofold throughout 1970–9, and is currently experiencing faster debt than GDP growth. Apart from Jamaica, which will be under IMF scrutiny for some time yet, two other countries in the sample — Bangladesh and Senegal — have no recourse except to emergency adjustments, including 'hyper-debt', external management of their national economies, and slow, zero, or negative economic growth.

If one bears in mind the manifestation, over the last two years, of the increasingly acrimonious relations between the United States and other OECD countries, and between Japan and other OECD countries (the United States through its monetarist and deflationary policies, and Japan through its mercantilism) it is easy to appreciate adjustment problems. But however painful the effects of small annual cuts in per capita GNP may be, these countries operate from a position of wealth, with mobile and dynamic financial and economic systems. The developing countries face adjustment from a greatly different stance — that of population growth, human needs, and development imperatives. The evidence of this chapter, therefore, is that North-controlled or dominated financial responses to developing country adjustment needs are confused. Large gaps in financing are increasingly evident, both for short-term, low-cost soft loans for balance of payments problems, and for long-term (perhaps more conditional) loans for development needs. The private-market recycling of petrodollars has not solved this problem, since the high-cost but unconditional loans that it provides are used to stem balance of payments problems rather than engage in major development projects.

Notes

1. H. Chenery *et al.*, *Patterns of Development*, Oxford, Oxford University Press, 1976.
2. Ibid.
3. See, for example, R. Triffin, 'Some observations on the geographical structure of deficits and their financing', *Pakistan Development Review*, Autumn 1979.
4. UNESCAP, 'Development strategies in the 1980s in the ESCAP region', *ad hoc* inter-governmental meeting on strategies for the 1980s, Bangkok, UNESCAP, August 1979.
5. *Financial Times*, London, 29 June 1981.
6. IBRD, *Energy in the Developing Countries*, Washington DC, IBRD, August 1980, p. 48.
7. Author's calculation.
8. IBRD, *Energy Prices, Substitution and Optimal Borrowing in the Short Run*, Washington DC, IBRD, July 1981.
9. Ibid.
10. UNCTAD/UNDP, *Balance of Payments Adjustment in Developing Countries*, Project INT. 75105, New York, UNCTAD/UNDP, 1979.
11. S. Jones, *International Monetary and Finance Issues and Developing Countries*, Sussex, Institute of Development Studies, 1980.
12. M. Cutajar, 'Background notes on the IMF', *Development Dialogue*, **2**, 1980.
13. Commonwealth Institute, *The World Economic Crisis*, Economic Paper 13, London, Commonwealth Secretariat, September 1980.
14. 'Causes authentiques et artificielles des défauts de paiements', *Le Monde*, Paris, 2 November 1982.
15. N. Girvan, 'Swallowing the IMF Medicine in the 1970s', *Development Dialogue*, **2**, 1980.
16. See Table 4.4.
17. W. Robichek, 'The IMF's experience in facilitating adjustment in the Commonwealth Caribbean', seminar on adjustment policies, London,

Commonwealth Institute, 27–30 April 1982.

18. IBRD, *Commodity Trade and Price Trends*, Washington DC, IBRD, August 1981.
19. See C. Blackwell, 'Reflections on the monetary approach to balance of payments', *IMF Survey*, 20 February and 6 March 1978.
20. See, for example, P. Saladin, 'The link between the creation of SDRs and development finance', *Development Dialogue*, **1**, 1981.
21. Commonwealth Institute, op. cit.
22. M. Desai, 'Effects of the rise in oil prices on South Asian countries, 1972–8', *ILO Review*, 120/2, March–April 1981.
23. Desai, 'Impact of higher oil prices on India', ILO Working Paper 50, Geneva, ILO-BIT WEPR, September 1979.
24. R. Islam, 'Some economic implications of higher oil prices: Bangladesh', ILO Working Paper 52, Geneva, WEPR, November 1979.
25. Desai, op. cit.

5 DEVELOPMENT, ENERGY, AND ADJUSTMENT TRENDS AND PROBLEMS IN DEVELOPING COUNTRIES

5.1 Introduction

The modern sector is advancing in all developing countries, and with it a tide of urbanisation. Again, this has major economic and energy demand implications. External and economic factors (here the focus is on adjustment and energy) have major implications for the role, size, and development of the modern sector

5.1.1 Agricultural development

It has already been noted that developing countries are far more dependent on food imports than on energy imports. Not, of course, in narrow financial terms, since food products have not in any way shown the pattern of price rises that petroleum, manufactured goods, or certain primary materials have shown. However, the developing countries, seen over a thirty-year span as in Table 5.1, have become more and more dependent on food imports. This has been partly due to a decline in real food prices, and consequently part of the developing world has slid to complete dependence for

Table 5.1 World grain trade patterns, 1934–1976

	Exports (+) or imports (−) (million tons)				
Region	1934-8 (average)	1948-52 (average)	1960	1970	1976
North America	+5	+23	+39	+56	+94
Latin America	+9	+1	0	+4	−3
Western Europe	−24	−22	−25	−30	−17
Eastern Europe and the USSR	+5	0	0	−1	−27
Africa	+1	0	−2	−5	−10
Asia	+2	−6	−17	−37	−47
Australia	+3	+3	+6	+12	+8

Source: L. Brown, *The Politics and Responsibility of the North American Breadbasket,* Paper 2, Washington DC, Worldwatch Institute, October 1976.

grains on the North American 'breadbasket'. While all the sample countries (except Kenya) import around 25 to 50 per cent of their calorie-supplying foods, such as wheat and rice, their role as a percentage of all merchandise imports has declined, despite rises in quantities. This is shown in Table 5.2, which compares food imports relative to all merchandise imports. As the last column in this table

Table 5.2 Food imports relative to all merchandise imports for each sample country, 1960 and 1978 (per cent)

Country	*1960*	*1970*	*Percentage of calorie needs relative to the WHO minimum* 1979*
Bangladesh	—	28	93
Sri Lanka	39	30	91
Kenya	12	7	91
Senegal	30	23	97
Peru	16	16	100
Jamaica	22	23	119

* IBRD calculation of total food supply relative to the minimum calorie needs of a population

Sources: IBRD, *World Development Report*, New York, Oxford University Press, 1978, 1979, 1980; and IBRD, *World Tables*, Baltimore, Johns Hopkins University Press, 1980.

indicates, only Peru (which as an oil exporter is now in a position to make large purchases of low-priced grains and can supply its population with the minimum calorie needs) and Jamaica (which has an excellent record of food supply on a calorie basis) are able to satisfy basic needs. For all other countries in the sample the food problem is increasing, particularly so for Bangladesh, which sets a minimum calorie needs standard significantly below the WHO standards. Bangladesh required as much as 51 per cent of its total imports as food in the bad year of 1975, and counts more than 70 per cent of its population as 'absolute poor', meaning that they are at an income level so low that purchases of even very small amounts of food are impossible.[1] The sample countries typically depict the increasing import-dependence for basic needs found in all developing countries.

Recalling the data presented in Section 3.3.1 on the potential net primary productivity of national ecosystems, it is remarkable how Kenya, Senegal, and Peru have drifted to a position of total dependence on basic food imports, while at the same time they are very large (Kenya and Senegal) or large (Peru) agricultural commodity and specialist food exporters. In terms of land resources, all these countries have the capacity to be large food exporters. Significantly, the member countries of the EEC respond as much to political pressures (notably from France, Italy, and Greece) as to strategic concerns for reducing food import-dependence, and since 1976 (the time of the data shown in Table 5.1) they have become small grain *exporters*. This has largely been achieved through the mobilisation of technological and capital resources rather than by the use of new land. This point can be better appreciated by a perception of the potential arable land available per continent, relative to actual agricultural usage, as shown in Table 5.3.

Table 5.3: Potential land available for farming relative to actual farm usage, 1960–1970, by continent (ratio)

Continent	*Ratio unused/used*
North America	49.51
Europe	12.88
Africa	78.22
South America	89.11
Australia, New Zealand	90.10
USSR	36.64
Asia, Middle East	17.83

Source: W.D. Hopper, 'The development of agriculture in developing countries', *Scientific American*, September 1976.

Thus, on a purely environmental and ecological basis, the two African countries and one South American country in the sample are very well endowed with the basic resources for agriculture. This, it should be noted, even applies to Senegal, despite the desertification that has severely affected much of its land resources. It is therefore in this sector of agricultural development (which of course includes rural development) that are found some of the greatest tensions between modernisation and efforts towards an overall improvement in human welfare. The crucial question thus becomes: at what rate should agricultural activity be replaced by industry, while maximising human welfare at minimum resource cost? Decision makers in developing countries, faced by a host of problems (such as economic adjustment), and by many costly non-problems, have tended to ignore the mounting food and rural development problem. This is shown by the sharp and consistent fall in the growth rates of agricultural output in all developing countries, particularly the poorer developing countries. It is especially marked in the poorer African countries, to such an extent that the director of the FAO (addressing the Twelfth Regional Conference of the FAO in 1982) remarked: 'Africa is sick, and its sole chance of recovery lies in very strong growth of its internal food production, and a continued increase in export receipts, notably in the agricultural sector.'[2]

The agricultural sector, of course, contains the crux of the problem. All four of the lower-income countries in this sample are major agricultural commodity exporters. It has already been noted that rapid terms of trade fluctuations, when superimposed on a structural pattern of decline, exert very strong negative adjustment influences, for example by attracting major investments (in a good year) that give poor returns (in a year of unfavourable terms of trade). Solving this problem demands not only a much greater willingness on the part of the national leaders of such countries to commit resources to basic development, but also an improved, stabilised, and rationalised price system for agricultural exports. Further, it is impossible to expect market forces in a country to shift production towards agriculture, when rural people are invariably the poorest group in an already very poor nation.

The food problem has become so serious in many African countries such as Senegal (and to some extent Kenya) that various actions, including the boycott of non-food agricultural exports, have been suggested by the North. A boycott of Senegal's agricultural exports was proposed by France during 1982. In response to this proposal The Dakar newspaper, *Le Soleil,* stated in its editorial (written by S. Gaye) that it admired such a gesture of international solidarity, but it also went on to remark:

> What would happen, in the case of a boycott, to the Senegalese economy if it was deprived overnight of export receipts from peanuts, the major crop? In a normal year peanut exports represent over 40% of total Senegalese trade receipts . . . 50% of agricultural receipts [and is the economic base] . . . of a national population that is more than 80% rural . . . Rather than a possible boycott on commercial export crops, to force African countries to revise their agricultural policies, would not Northern

solidarity with Third World problems be better expressed through a consensus on [prices for] agricultural primary product exports?[3]

As Gaye further remarked, the primary commodity export system, which does not yield food for local consumption, is part of an international, and unequal, pattern of trade relations. While, theoretically, the alternative of political action is open to developing countries in this situation, the number of leaders prepared to take such action, whatever their political persuasion, can be counted on the fingers of very few hands. Thus, in a very real way, the rural poor of developing countries represent the 'human subsidy' to both their own, and international, patterns of 'development', patterns which after the two oil crises have become less able to conceal this exploitation.

The energy sector is directly linked to the problem of increasing rural poverty, and to that of agricultural growth rates which are wholly unable to keep pace with population growth, let alone support real improvements in human welfare. As the cost of commercial energy supplies mounts, even with the subsidisation that is criticised by the IBRD, IMF, and other institutions, the pressure on non-commercial energy supplies increases relentlessly. Many studies have described this problem,[4] which contributes very significantly to the mounting loss of cropland, estimated at about 6 million hectares per annum in Africa.[5] Only through rapidly accelerated rural development, and almost certainly through rapid rises in rural cash incomes, can this negative trend be halted and, finally, reversed. In reality, the loss of cropland through the 'predatory' use of non-commercial energy fuel resources by people too poor to buy even the cheapest and most efficient household cooking equipment is both a tragic waste of human and economic resources, and the destruction of future national capital.

The comments of the director-general of the FAO,[6] and those of M. Gaye[7] of *Le Soleil*, underline the most basic need of developing countries, which is the stabilisation, with an underlying upward trend, of agricultural commodity prices. Without this there is no possibility — except, for example, the discovery of very high-value mineral commodities — for rural development in the vast majority of developing countries, nor in all the low-income countries featured in this study.

5.2 Industrial development

The conclusion reached in the preceding section is strongly supported by the major trends in industrial development in most developing countries, and by the economic performance of the sample countries. Three major trends can be identified, namely:

(i) rapid population growth;
(ii) rapid urbanisation; and
(iii) increasing capital-intensity of industry.

Again, these factors have major energy implications, and are also significantly time-dependent. According to the IBRD, and using quite optimistic projections of the annual decrease in population growth rate relative to growth of income, all the sample countries will require at least twenty years (Jamaica), and many up to fifty-five years (Bangladesh, Kenya, and Senegal), before they reach stable (zero growth) population. By this time, the total 1979 population of the sample group (about 146 million) will have grown to about 565 million.[8] This alone gives an added dimension to the need for stabilised, and subsequently increased food production.

With regard to factor (ii), all the sample countries have experienced very high growth rates of urban population. These ranged from nearly 7 per cent per annum for Bangladesh to 3.3 per cent per annum for Senegal, throughout the 1970s. The rate of urbanisation was at least 1.5 times that of national income growth. It is only necessary to appreciate that the use of certain non-commercial energy fuels (crop residues and dung) is becoming increasingly difficult for urban populations, and that wood fuel use is constrained by urban transport limitations, to understand that urbanisation is itself a factor pushing the populations of developing countries towards the use of commercial energy. Of course, this energy does not necessarily have to be petroleum-based, or even (in theory) mineral-based. But, prior to the development of indigenous energy infrastructures, it is obvious that urbanisation implies an inherent trend towards greater use of commercial energy.

Factor (iii), increasing capital-intensity of industry, is perhaps the most important, at least in relation to economic adjustment over the coming decade. A recent study by the ILO, for example, notes that the proportion of the labour force engaged in manufacturing in Bangladesh and the Philippines *fell* quite considerably (by about 30 per cent) between 1957 and 1972, while in the same period the contribution of industry to GDP increased by about 20 per cent. The report commented: 'The use of labour-saving technology has resulted in chronically slow rates of job creation in the modern sector. As the case studies [of certain Asian developing countries] demonstrate, this has meant a worsening of unemployment and underemployment.' [9]

Table 5.4: Labour allocation in relation to population and GDP growth in each sample country, 1960–1979

	Percentage of labour force in:						*Population growth (per cent)*	*Real GDP growth (per cent)**
	Agriculture		*Industry*		*Services*			
Country	1960	1979	1960	1979	1960	1979	1960-79	1960-79
Bangladesh	87	74	3	11†	10	15	157	76
Sri Lanka	56	54	14	14	30	32	43	97
Kenya	86	78	5	10	9	12	72	154
Senegal	84	76	5	10	11	14	53	60
Peru	53	38	19	20	28	42	58	93
Jamaica	39	22	25	25	36	53	33	47

* GDP growth quantities for 1960–79 are calculated using the annualised growth shown in Table 2 of the IBRD *World Development Report* of 1981.

† Data for Bangladesh incorporate classifications different from many other countries.

Source: IBRD, *World Development Report*, 1981, Tables 2 and 17.

The pattern of labour allocation in relation to population and GDP growth in the sample countries during the period 1960–79 is shown in Table 5.4. It is significant that, excluding Bangladesh, only two sample countries (Kenya and Senegal) showed a growth in the industrial share of the labour forces greater than population growth. In Peru, Jamaica, and Sri Lanka the proportion of the labour force in industry was virtually static, despite the large growth of GDP. On the other hand, nearly all the countries in the sample, despite their very large agricultural labour forces, were either already very large food importers (Bangladesh, Sri Lanka, and Senegal), or were rapidly increasing their food imports (Kenya). Furthermore, in these countries the share of manufacturing in the industrial sector, which is typically 50 to 75 per cent of all industry, produces very much more value-added per worker than the agricultural sector. For example, manufacturing employment in Sri Lanka acounts for about 65 per cent of the industrial sector, which in 1979 employed (see Table 5.4) 14 per cent of the labour force. Yet in the same year the 54 per cent of the labour force engaged in agriculture produced only 1.3 times more output than the (approximately) 9 per cent of the labour force in manufacturing.

Using IBRD data, the ratio of agricultural to manufacturing output, measured as shares of GDP, is shown for each sample country in Table 5.5 and Figure 5.1. These data indicate trends that allow the sample countries to be divided into two categories based on their

Table 5.5: Ratio of agricultural output to manufacturing output, as proportions of GDP for each sample country, selected years, 1970–1979

Country	*1970*	*1972*	*1973*	*1974*	*1976*	*1978*	*1979*
Bangladesh	8.7	14.3	8.6	8.3	7.6	7.1	7.0
Sri Lanka	2.8	2.4	2.5	3.4	2.6	1.5	1.3
Kenya	2.8	2.7	2.5	2.3	2.6	3.4	3.8
Senegal	1.8	2.0	1.7	2.0	2.1	1.4	1.5
Peru	1.1	1.0	0.9	0.8	0.8	0.6	0.4
Jamaica	0.4	0.4	0.4	0.4	0.5	0.5	0.5

Source: Derived from IBRD, World Tables, 1980, 'Economic data sheet 1' for relevant countries; and IBRD, *World Development Report,* 1980, 1981.

GNP income group. For the two richest developing countries in the sample (Peru and Jamaica) the lower agricultural proportion of the labour force is directly reflected in the low contribution of agriculture relative to manufacturing, when compared with the other sample countries. The marked contraction of the Jamaican economy throughout the period 1976–9 has, however, reversed a downward, or stabilised, pattern of agricultural output relative to manufacturing output. The initial change (shown in Figure 5.1), which occurred around 1974–5, can easily be traced to Jamaica's short sugar boom. The maintenance of the relatively higher proportion of agriculture in GDP after this time can be attributed to the fact that manufacturing output was contracting faster than agricultural output.

For the other sample countries, all heavily dependent on primary commodity exports, the small proportion of the labour force engaged in manufacturing (around 6 to 9 per cent) was producing about 2.5 times more output per worker than the larger agricultural proportion (about 54 to 78 per cent) in 1979. However, the strong

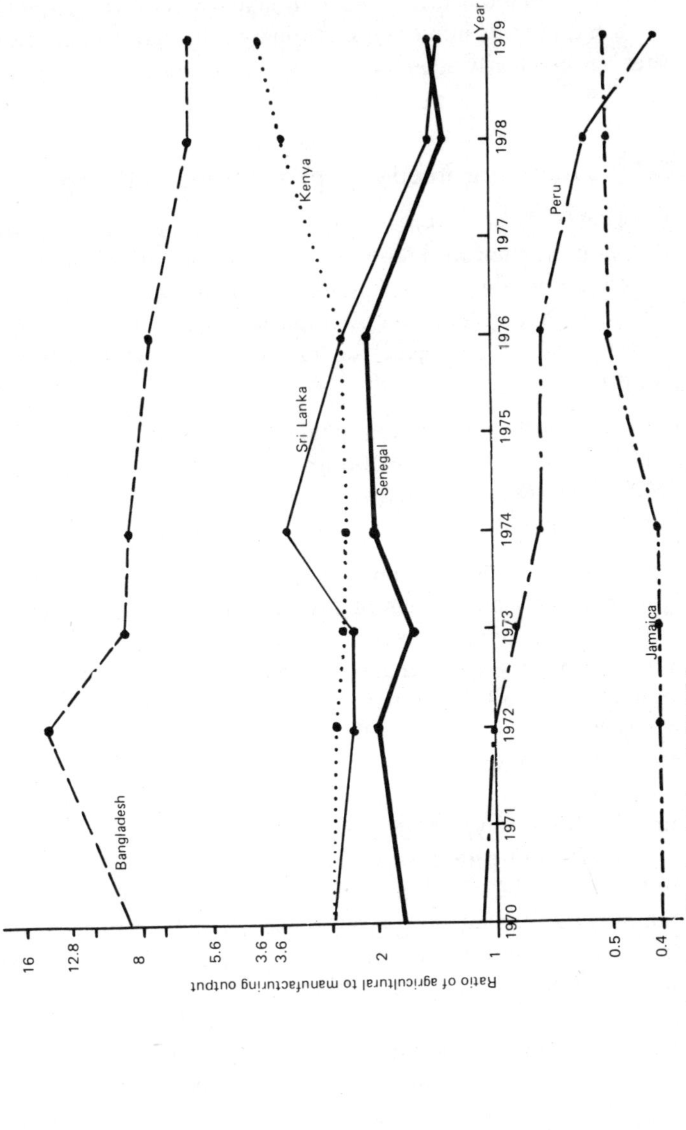

* Based on data shown in Table 5.5

Fig. 5.1 Ratio of agricultural output to manufacturing output, as proportions of GDP, for each sample country, 1970–1979* dominance of primary commodities, including major non-food agricultural commodities in the case of Kenya (for example pyrethrum), is shown by the fact that for these countries in 1979 the agricultural sector was 1.5 to 7 times more important, on a GDP basis, than manufacturing. As with Jamaica, the strong influence of the terms of trade movements is apparent in all these countries, and this can be clearly seen by comparing Figure 5.1 with Figures 3.2 and 3.3.

5.3 Financing needs — projections and gaps

It has already been noted (Section 4.2) that the IBRD 'high case' (1980) projection for increased GNP growth of developing countries incorporates certain assumptions of capital needs, growth rates, and dependence on oil imports. As is well known from the literature on this subject, the rate of economic growth for any country:

(i) increases with the marginal savings ratio;
(ii) varies with the capital-output ratio;
(iii) is decreased by high interest/debt costs; and
(iv) varies with the conditonality, etc. of loans.

Essentially, developing countries pass through a phase when debt grows faster than savings or investment, into a more developed phase, when savings not only cover investment but also yield a surplus for cancelling external debt. The great majority of developing countries in the 1970s expanded debt obligations much faster than GDP. By analysis of the GDP growth, investment, and debt structures of the sample countries it is possible to make certain projections of the gaps in financing. These projections, it must be understood, are hypothetical, and are provided only for illustration.

The UNIDO projections of investment finance needs [10] relate only to the industrial sector, and are very highly aggregated. Thus the only two capital–output ratios used —0.49 for poorer developing countries and 0.46 for middle-income developing countries — do not take account of country-wide performance. Such an approach, which assumes that poorer developing countries and middle-income developing countries place, respectively, 1.36 and 1.18 times as much capital into direct investment as into non-productive investment (training, infrastructure, etc.), ignores very great variations from country to country. Where industrialisation is weak (as for most of the sample countries), or the industrial sector is highly energy-intensive (Jamaica), or a large proportion of national investment goes to essentially unproductive sectors (for example Peru's arms purchases), the capital–output ratio can fall far below that used by UNIDO. This is further reinforced by social, human, geographical, and other factors. Thus large developing countries (including the three of this sample) with low levels of human development, such as in literacy and health care, must devote large sums to these uses, unproductive though they may be in the short run.

The capital–output ratio for the sample countries as shown in Table 5.6, are calculated using data for the period 1973–9 as the base. This period includes the first oil crisis, and at least one year of the second, and provides data sources that have improved with time throughout the decade 1970–80. Only Bangladesh shows a capital–output ratio close to the UNIDO figure cited earlier. The

Table 5.6: Real growth in GDP and Gross Domestic Investment (GDI) 1973–1979, and the capital–output ratio, for each sample country

Country	*Real growth of GDP 1973–9 (per cent)*	*Annualised average growth of GDP 1973–9 (per cent)*	*GDI as a percentage of GDP (average) 1973–9*	*Capital–output ratio*
Bangladesh	31.7	5.28	9.7	0.54
Sri Lanka	29.1	4.85	18.5	0.26
Kenya	33.2	5.53	23.8	0.23
Senegal	24.4	4.07	19.5	0.21
Peru	15.3	2.55	16.7	0.15
Jamaica (1960–79)	47.0	2.04	18.3	0.11

Source: Author's calculations, based on IBRD sources.

low capital–output ratios of the sample countries (which means that high investment increments are needed to return each extra unit of GDP) have important implications for the analysis of finance gaps in developing countries. These finance gaps are indicated in the projections shown in Table 5.7. In this table it is assumed that the target growth of GDP has to be modest (except for Bangaldesh) over the next nineteen years (1983–2002). Notably, the projected GDP growth rates avoid the euphoric projections of the Lima

Plan,[11] which sought a growth of 390 per cent in the GDP of developing countries from 1980–2000. Apart from being overtaken by events, this target has important defects in relation to the energy sector.

Table 5.7: Finance gaps for a real-growth scenario of each sample country, 1983–2002

Country	*Bangladesh*	*Sri Lanka*	*Kenya*	*Senegal*	*Peru*	*Jamaica*
Target annual GDP growth (per cent)	4.9	3.6	5.0	2.9	3.5	2.0
Real annual debt service growth (per cent)	5.8	7.3	7.6	26.9	14.1	18.1
Investment finance needs (as a percentage of GDP)	9.1	13.9	21.7	13.9	23.3	18.2
Marginal savings rate (per cent)	0	1.9	2.2	6.0	2.3	1.5
Net investment finance need (as a percentage of GDP)	14.9	19.3	27.3	34.7	35.1	34.8
GDI (as a percentage of GDP)	9.7	18.5	23.8	19.5	16.7	18.3
Imputed gap (as a percentage of GDP)	5.2	0.8	4.3	15.2	18.4	16.5

Source: Author's calculations, based on IBRD data and country data from official sources.

The GDP growth targets (expressed in real GDP terms) shown in Table 5.7 are identical to the annual GDP growth rates for the sample countries in 1969–79, except for Bangladesh and Senegal. It should be noted that during the 1970s three of the sample countries recorded annual average decreases in their GDP per capita. The GDP annual growth targets used in these projections are in all cases above population growth, and for Bangladesh and Senegal they are projected at 100 per cent and 50 per cent respectively above their 1960–79 average real GDP growths.

5.4 Development and energy

The importance of energy to national development, largely ignored during the cheap-energy era, threatens to become overexaggerated in the future. The more energy-intensive economies (by and large) of the industrial countries, where there is a relative shortage of large-scale, undeveloped energy resources, have coloured the analysis and appreciation of energy.

The process of development leads to a sharp increase in demand for commercial energy, which describes an arc from low-income/ low-energy economies, through fast-growing/high-energy economies, to the developed state of slow-growing (or even contracting) high-income economies which use an intermediate amount of commercial energy per unit of GDP. As will be seen in Chapter 6, various 'new wisdoms' have evolved over recent years to challenge this picture. They argue that lower-income developing countries derive a 'huge energy subsidy', particularly from their use of non-commercial energy, despite the extremely low levels of efficiency of such energy sources and systems.

Significantly, it is only in the two high-income (formerly 'fast-growing middle-income') countries of the sample that commercial energy intensities are found that are above those of the OECD countries. This can be seen from the data presented in Table 5.8. Once more, it is important to note that different data bases have major impacts on analyses and results and, consequently, on the

Table 5.8: Commercial energy intensities and boe* per $US1,000 for each sample country and all industrial countries, 1979.

Country	*GDP per capita (1979$US)*	*Commercial energy use (kgce per capita)*	*GDP output per boe (1979 $US)*	*boe commercial energy use per $US1,000 of GDP*
Bangladesh †	86	43	441	2.27
Sri Lanka	190	109	383	2.61
Kenya	345	180	421	2.37
Senegal	450	260	382	2.62
Peru	864	730	260	3.85
Jamaica	1,086	1,575	151	6.60
Federal Republic of Germany	12,483	6,627	414	2.41
All industrial countries	9,622	7,892	267	3.75

* boe — barrels oil equivalent.
† The data for Sri Lanka are for 1978.

Source: Author's calculations using IBRD data, and the energy equivalence of 1 barrel oil equivalent = 6.3GJ/6 million BTU/1,758 kWh.

conclusions that can be drawn. As this study has constantly pointed out, the approach of the IBRD towards adjustment pressures and responses is a major determinant, on the world scene, of the attitudes adopted by private financial institutions towards developing countries. Where a developing country finds itself in hyper-debt, and is lent IMF funds (which are conditional), the IBRD/IMF viewpoint on adjustment becomes paramount, at least for that country.

The IBRD *World Development Report* of 1981 is preoccupied by energy, and by the role and impact of energy in developing countries. Somewhat dubious price elasticity functions, and GDP growth elasticities relative to oil price increases, have been developed by the IBRD. In the 1981 *World Development Report* the IBRD comments on the OECD's success in energy adjustment, as shown by certain long-term price elasticity functions (which are higher than developing countries') and income elasticities (which are lower). The IBRD says:

> *The industrial countries.* Both GDP and energy use were increasing at about 5% per year before 1973, and the average intensity of their energy use was relatively constant at 5.0 barrels oil equivalent per $1000 of GDP. In the absence of any increase in prices, energy consumption would have risen to 117 million boe/day by 1990. Because of the dramatic price increases, however, energy intensities have fallen from 5 boe/$1000 of GDP in 1973, to 4.4 boe/$1000 in 1980. This implies a medium-term elasticity of about 0.2.[12]

Nowhere in the surrounding text from which this quotation is taken is there any reference to the year to which these data relate (which is 1979–80), nor is there any indication that the IBRD is using a 1975 dollar value when quoting 1980 data. However, the figure given (4.4 barrels oil equivalent (boe) per $US1,000 of GDP) is about 17 per cent bigger than that for 1979 as shown in Table 5.8, which uses the same data from the same IBRD report. The report, which discusses European and American adjustment, unveils the prospect of the North needing only 3.7 boe per $US1,000 of GDP in 1990, which is this study's assessment of the industrial countries' energy use in 1979.

These lapses are perhaps not of central importance, except to the extent that they make it very difficult to correlate IBRD data with those of this study. Proceeding to the analysis of Table 5.8, which uses explicit and quantified data bases, it is noticeable that four of the sample countries have commercial energy intensities far below the commercial energy intensity of all industrial countries and close to that of the Federal Republic of Germany, which has one of the world's most highly developed industrial economies. Conversely, the high and growing commercial energy intensity of Peru demonstrates the very high but stable energy phase of developing countries when passing from the low-income, low-energy stage of development (characterised by the dominance of agricultural export commodities) to economies where manufacturing begins to play a major role, at least equal to that of agriculture.

In an energy context, the very high energy 'efficiency' of the first four sample countries in Table 5.8 directly supports the argument that such countries can readily use much more commercial energy. It is here that stabilised financial conditions and more-organised and stable patterns of commodity prices, plus a better appreciation of long-term capital investment needs versus short-term adjustment loans to balance trade and current account deficits, are strongly indicated.

However, many infrastructural investments are of necessity highly energy-intensive, and this problem is reinforced by urbanisation as well as by industrialisation. For these reasons, the energy sector in development and adjustment cannot be ignored, but calls for:

(i) cost-effective development of indigenous energy;
(ii) sectoral choices based at least partly on energy input per unit of GDP; and
(iii) national energy planning agencies able to co-ordinate multi-sectorial energy programmes.

This need is increasingly recognised in the developing countries,[13] but to date there is no conclusive evidence of this recognition being followed by concise and effective action. Several energy sector problems, especially those concerning the allocation of scarce national resources to this sector, can be evoked. The role and scope of household and non-commercial energy within national development can also be singled out as being of great importance, certainly for two or three of the countries in this sample. These and other points are discussed further in Chapter 6.

Notes

1. UNESCAP, 'Development strategies in the 1980s in the ESCAP region', *ad hoc* inter-governmental meeting on strategies for the 1980s, Bangkok, UNESCAP, August 1979.
2. *Le Monde,* Paris, 9 October 1982.
3. S. Gaye, *Le Soleil,* Dakar, reproduced in *Le Monde,* Paris, 7 October 1982.
4. *Le Monde,* Paris, 9 October 1982.
5. See, for example, R. Caceras, 'Wood-saving stoves in Guatemala', in CENRENEIO, *Seminar on New and Renewable Sources of Energy,* Oxford, CENRENEIO, October 1981.
6. *Le Monde,* Paris, 9 October 1982.
7. Gaye, op. cit.
8. IBRD, *World Development Report,* New York, Oxford University Press, 1981, Table 17.
9. ILO-BIT, *Profiles of Rural Poverty,* Geneva, World Employment Program, ILO-BIT, 1979.
10. UNIDO, *The Impact of Higher Energy Prices on the Industrialisation of Developing Countries,* Paper IS279, Vienna, UNIDO, January 1982, p. 27 citing, *inter alia,* J. Stern 'The employment impact of industrial investment', IBRD Working Paper 255, Washington DC, IBRD, June 1977.
11. UNIDO, *Second Conference on Industrialisation,* Lima, UNIDO, 1974.
12. IBRD, *World Development Report,* 1981, pp. 35–8.
13. See, for example, S. Al-Shaikhly and M. Ul-Haq, 'Energy and development', *8th Roundtable Conference on Energy and Economic Development,* Paper 2, Washington DC, NRST-SID, October 1980.

6 THE ROLE AND PERSPECTIVE OF OIL IMPORTS AND ADJUSTMENT

6.1 Introduction

It has been maintained in this study that, even allowing for the two oil crises, the role of oil imports in the financial and development problems of developing countries has been exaggerated: In conventional analyses of the adjustment process undue emphasis has been placed on just one component — oil imports — because of its 'visibility'. Institutions such as the IBRD and the IMF have, in particular, suggested a direct link between petroleum imports and the financial problems of developing countries. Another frequent argument is that 'non-commercial energy' can be readily equated with modern commercial energy. By this reasoning, many developing countries appear to be very 'inefficient' in their gross use of energy relative to GDP.

Both of these views are challenged in this study. From the analysis in this chapter and elsewhere in the study it is suggested that two general trends appear to be in operation for at least the majority of the sample countries. These trends are:

(i) a fairly small but continuing increase in per capita use of commercial energy; and
(ii) a marked economy in the use of commercial energy by comparison with the energy-based economic performance of the OECD countries.

The problems of adjustment, which in essence are financial problems of (hopefully) a short-term nature, have had major effects on the commercial energy trends in the sample countries. Most of the sample countries have shown rapid changes in commercial energy use related to annual variations in GDP. Also, most of the sample countries have shown steady increases in national production of commercial energy, one of the major recommendations for adjustment as defined by the 'central hypothesis'. This study therefore concludes that, in the energy sector, at least the sample countries have shown their desire to adjust, but it also concludes that this sector cannot be dissociated from the rest of the economy, or from the international context.

6.2 The energy sector

It is customary, when describing the energy sector of developing countries, to note the predominance of petroleum and the high growth rates of demand for this fuel. The predominance of petroleum in the total commercial energy use of the sample countries is shown in Table 6.1. Several major factors in this overall trend towards high dependence on petroleum will be noted later.

Table 6.1 Approximate role of petroleum in the total commercial energy use of each sample country, date of estimate indicated (per cent)

	*Bangladesh**	*SriLanka**	*Kenya †*	*Senegal ‡*	*Peru§*	*Jamaica ¶*
Date of estimate	1978	1978	1979	1976	1976	1978
Petroleum as a percentage of total commercial energy use	50.5	90.3	88.2	100	83.1	98.7

Sources: * UNESCAP, *Short-term Economic Policy Aspects of the Energy Situation in the ESCAP Region*, Bangkok, UNESCAP, 1981.
† UNDP/IBRD, *Kenya — Issues and Options in the Energy Sector*, Report 3800-KE, Washington DC, IBRD, 1981.
‡ From the data bank on ACP states, EEC Directorate-General for Development, Brussels.
§ US Department of Energy, *Joint US/Peru Report on Peru*, co-operative assessment project, Washington DC, 1979.
¶ Ministry of Mining and Energy, *Jamaica National Energy Plan*, Kingston, 1981.

However, the data do not support the frequently cited 'high growth rates' of demand for commercial energy (and therefore petroleum) in developing countries such as those of the sample. As is shown in Table 6.2, commercial energy trends in the sample countries show that there has been a good level of general adjustment in the commercial energy sector in response to the continuing rise in energy prices. In addition, those countries with low or very low per capita commercial energy consumption have not shown large increases in demand. The data used for Table 6.2 suffer from the weaknesses noted elsewhere concerning the accuracy and consistency of energy data for the developing countries. However, it is obvious that the sample group shows a distinct post-oil crisis trend of much greater increases in commercial energy production relative to commercial energy consumption. This is also apparent in the special case of Jamaica, the most energy- and petroleum-intensive economy of the sample. This general trend, only absent in the case of Senegal, can easily be described as 'adjustment' according to the concepts advanced by the IBRD.

Table 6.2 Long-run per capita commercial energy growth rates (post-1974 production and consumption changes) for each sample country (annual average, per cent)

Factor	*Bangladesh*	*Sri Lanka*	*Kenya*	*Senegal*	*Peru*	*Jamaica*
1960-78 per capita commercial energy consumption	n/a*	+0.2	+1.3	+2.3	+2.1	+15.0
Commercial energy production change 1974-9	+10.8	+8.5	+17.5	0	+18.4	−2.0
Commercial energy consumption change 1974-9	+6.3	+3.8	+3.5	+12.4	+2.7	−5.4

* n/a — no available data.

Source: IBRD, *World Development Report*, New York, Oxford University Press, 1980, 1981.

In relation to per capita commercial energy growth rates, all of sample countries except Jamaica have shown rather weak growth, which conflicts with the conventional image of 'extreme' or 'very rapid' growth of commercial energy (and therefore petroleum) demand in developing countries. Jamaica does not conform with this trend of low growth in per capita commercial energy consumption (from base levels of demand that are, typically, one-tenth to one-twentieth of the average for all developing countries) for special reasons. These relate to the arrival in the early 1960s of world-class alumina production, an industry that is extremely energy-intensive. If the commercial energy use of the bauxite and alumina industry in Jamaica is removed from the analysis, per capita consumption levels, and growth rates of personal energy demand, are shown to be over 60 per cent lower than their present levels.

Most of the sample countries have shown a marked variability in commercial energy consumption trends since the first oil crisis. By comparison with the commercial energy trends of all the developing countries, the performance of the sample group has shown very large variations. The sample consists of six, small, oil-importing countries whose characteristics reflect the majority of developing countries. However, the *overall* trends of all developing countries reflect the economic characteristics of the energy sector of the eight largest oil importers. These, together with the five main developing countries which export refined petroleum products, imported some 87 per cent of *total* developing country oil imports in 1979.[1] The 'Big-Eight', which include India, Brazil, and South Korea, are essentially powerful, often dynamic, industrialising countries, which have paid little heed to reducing petroleum imports and have concentrated on achieving rapid economic growth.

The four small oil-importing countries of the sample (Bangladesh, Sri Lanka, Kenya, and Senegal), and to some extent the more energy-intensive countries with higher GNP per capita (Jamaica and Peru), share certain common characteristics. These, as has been noted in the preceding chapters, tend to be characteristics shared by the majority of developing countries. They can be described in summary as:

(i) Developing countries with relatively small levels of industrialisation, dependent on primary product exports, and very strongly affected by the external economic environment, in particular the trend of world market prices for their primary exports.
(ii) This dependence on fluctuating terms of trade is reflected in rapid fluctuations in GDP growth rates, in the levels of economic activity, and thus in the levels of energy imports.
(iii) Commercial energy use is highly variable according to economic performance, and is further used at very different per capita rates according to social class.
(iv) The lower-income developing countries in particular show very high out-turns of GDP per unit commercial energy use, relative to middle-income developing countries and the OECD countries.

As noted in the analysis of commercial energy trends for the sample countries, the variations in terms of trade generally showed a good correlation with changes in commercial energy use. The general, rapid improvement in primary product prices from 1974 to 1976–7 was reflected in generally high growth rates of commercial energy consumption in those years. Equally, sharp decreases in export receipts (for example in Kenya from 1973–4) led to rapid decreases in the growth rates of commercial energy use. This pattern of change is not similar to that shown by the OECD countries in the same period.[2] The pattern of commercial energy consumption changes in the developing countries can be described as more abrupt, even 'brutal'.

Further, for most of the countries in the sample the period from 1974–9 was marked by significantly larger growth rates in commercial energy production relative to commercial energy consumption. Variability of demand, together with the trend of increased indigenous commercial energy production, are evidence of a pattern of changes in the energy sector that clearly demonstrates that adjustment is taking place.

It is obvious that sudden doublings or treblings in the ratio of the value of oil imports to total imports (see Table 4.4) must have a rapid downward impact on oil import demand. However, the high marginal utility of increased commercial energy use, and the low initial levels of per capita energy use, will result in a sharp upturn in demand for commercial energy whenever economic recovery takes place. Thus, when adverse terms of trade result in relatively large falls in net export receipts and produce quite large falls in GDP (expressed in constant currency units), the annual changes in commercial energy consumption tend to be large.

It is a central tenet of the 'conventional hypothesis' that the developing countries, in general, show high growth rates of petroleum demand and high marginal propensity to commercial energy consumption.[3] This does not, however, take account of the responsiveness of commercial energy demand to changes in GDP growth rates. This responsiveness, shown by very rapid annual changes in commercial energy demand, is such that advocates of the free play of market forces, such as the IBRD and IMF, should acknowledge it with approval.

Further analysis of the sample group reveals a linkage between the capital intensity of the economy and energy-related economic performance. If the capital-output ratio is related to the commercial energy intensity of the economy (as in Table 6.3) a clear and marked correlation is found. This directly supports the argument advanced so far in this chapter that the poorer developing countries (showing high capital–output ratios) utilise commercial energy very efficiently. The data in Table 6.3 support the argument that increased industrialisation and urbanisation need more commercial

Table 6.3 The capital–output ratio and commercial energy intensity* for each sample country, 1970–1979

Country	*Capital–output ratio (average 1970–79)*	*Commercial energy intensity 1979*
Bangladesh	0.54	2.27
Sri Lanka	0.26	2.61
Kenya	0.23	2.37
Senegal	0.21	2.62
Peru	0.15	3.86
Jamaica	0.11	6.60

* Measured as the ratio of barrels oil equivalent (boe) per $US1,000 of GDP, 1979.

Source: Author's calculations, based on IBRD sources. See Tables 5.6 and 5.8.

energy because they establish economic structures which are characterised by greater organisation and rigidity in energy use. The development of infrastructures, greater industrial activity, and an increase in socio-economic development all lead to higher base levels of energy demand. Because of the increase in capital intensity, more investment is needed per unit increase of GDP output and, generally, more commercial energy is required per unit of GDP. Thus the implication of economic development is that countries do not have the flexibility to make a rapid decrease, or increase, in commercial energy use in response to GDP growth rates.

These changes in the energy economy, which have been observed in the sample group and in developing countries generally, can be summarised as follows:

(i) low-income developing countries generally have simple, rugged, and highly flexible commercial energy systems with, typically, low maintenance costs;
(ii) the energy sector in low-income developing countries must show high returns on equity investment to attract scarce private or state capital; and
(iii) these factors tend to confine the effective choice of energy systems to low-cost, profitable, petroleum-based systems with low maintenance costs.

Many other factors support this general conclusion. For example, developing countries of large geographical spread or low population density (like three of the countries in this sample), and with a significant emphasis on agriculture, can only achieve electrification at high social cost. The problems of developing non-petroleum-based energy systems are further increased by the general lack of skilled manpower and by the role of private capital in development.

On the other hand, a developing country importing refined petroleum products for direct end-use needs only a simple infrastructure of storage and distribution. The cost of establishing more capital-intensive electrical power systems which can use a range of primary sources (hydro, coal, nuclear, gas, oil, and some renewables) can be appreciated from the large economic demands made by electrification. For those developing countries that have chosen the nuclear option, this choice often demands 10 to 15 per cent of the country's entire trained manpower, and as much as 50 per cent of all energy sector spending, to yield no more than 0.5 to 1 per cent of total commercial energy.[4] Most developing countries devote over a third of all energy investment to electrical power, while obtaining only about 10 to 15 per cent of total commercial energy from electricity.[5]

There are obvious problems for developing countries in a petroleum-dominated commercial energy system. One such problem is the mounting cost of using petroleum for energy alone, when petroleum is also an important base for petrochemicals. Another is that in the often small and fragmented markets of developing countries, the function of two, three, or four or more local affiliates of the international majors can often be that of inefficient monopolistic competition rather than the provision of a least-cost service to the consumer. And while the flexibility and low maintenance costs of oil-based energy systems mean that large fluctuations in energy demand can be easily accommodated, the establishment of more organised, but still flexible, power systems based on this fuel is more difficult. One reason for this is the inefficient transportation of oil products over long distances for end-uses that might, with investment, be served by locally generated electricity.

The major factors at play affecting the choice and speed of energy sector, and economic, development can be summarised as follows:

(i) the stabilisation or increase of per capita commercial energy demand (with a proportional upward trend for economic and demographic growth) is required for the development of the energy sector;

(ii) the electrical power sector, though capital-intensive, provides versatility in the choice of primary energy sources; and

(iii) monopolistic competition in the supply/distribution of petroleum can entail large additional costs, and thus may require greater regulation, or nationalisation.

6.3 Role of petroleum imports in adjustment

It has already been noted in Chapters 3 and 4 that increased spending on imports of all kinds has a major impact on trade balances and the current account. In turn, this affects the pace and structure of economic growth. However, the concepts advanced by those analysts of adjustment who attribute most of the adjustment problems of developing countries to the petroleum factor are not reflected in the trends. Thus, the IBRD's recent analysis[6] of the adjustment problem of all developing countries (considered as a group) arrives at the conclusion that the 'final form of adjustment' — deflation of the economy — is inevitable. In this study's analysis of a sample of smaller developing countries, which is probably more representative of all developing countries than are the large oil consumers, it is found that the financial impact of large oil prices rises was mitigated in those countries showing consistent growth in export values. On the other hand, adjustment was made more difficult where merchandise deficits continued to rise after the first oil crisis. To illustrate this process, the period from 1973–7, for three of the sample countries, is shown in Table 6.4 which covers petroleum imports, trade, and trade deficits. Broadly speaking, Bangladesh and Jamaica, together with Senegal (and Peru until 1978–9), showed a pattern of deteriorating export performance and increasing trade deficits. In this nexus the role of increased petroleum spending sharpened an already very unfavourable situation. On the other hand, Sri Lanka and Kenya showed a pattern of sharply reducing trade deficits (despite increased petroleum imports) due to rapid gains in favourable price movements for their primary product exports. To a certain extent all the sample countries have shown this last pattern, but only for a limited period within the study. This includes Jamaica in 1974–6, Senegal in 1972–4, and Peru in 1978–80, and in all cases it was due to a reversal of the unfavourable trend in terms of trade.

Table 6.4 Petroleum imports and other trade balances for Bangladesh, Kenya, and Sri Lanka, 1973–1977 (current $US)

Factor	*Bangladesh*					*Kenya*					*Sri Lanka*				
	1973	1974	1975	1976	1977	1973	1974	1975	1976	1977	1973	1974	1975	1976	1977
Total merchandise trade ($US millions)	1,148	1,340	1,484	1,185	1,516	1,015	1,479	1,490	1,555	2.263	738	1,138	1,237	1,132	1,394
Deficit on merchandise trade ($US millions)	432	644	886	342	564	75	317	224	62.5	13	5	120	125	19	+102
Petroleum imports* ($US millions)	27.8	86	342	235	245	1.2	36	37.5	35	33.8	48	147	137	151	176
Change (+ or −) in petroleum imports, by value, on preceding year (per cent) †	+36	+209	+298	−32	+4	+6.5	+276	+18	−8	+12	+54	+208	−7	+10	+17

* Net imports. In the cases of Bangladesh and Sri Lanka, petroleum exports/re-exports are either zero or very small. In the case of Kenya, however, petroleum product re-exports to dependent consumer hinterlands were important trade items until 1973, and almost covered the entire cost of petroleum imports

† In the case of Kenya, the annual change in the percentage value of petroleum imports is shown on the base of *total* petroleum imports, not net imports.

Sources: UNESCAP, 'Development strategies in the 1980s in the ESCAP region', *ad hoc* inter-governmental meeting on strategies for the 1980s, Bangkok, UNESCAP, August 1979; UNDP/IBRD, *Kenya — Issues and Options in the Energy Sector;* and IBRD, *World Tables,* Baltimore, Johns Hopkins University Press, 1980.

When other important financial factors are added to the analysis, notably aid, concessionary loans, and workers' remittances from oil-exporting countries, it becomes still harder to describe the role of oil imports in adjustment as uniqely important or as its basic cause. Rather, the sudden increase in oil prices in the first oil crisis period of 1973–4 helped, perhaps, to dramatise the more general economic and development problems of many developing countries. These problems, which have been noted throughout this study, include dependence on primary product exports (and thus extreme exposure to terms of trade changes), and an infrastructure inadequately developed to meet the very high costs of developing alternatives in the energy sector. It is here sufficient to note that the 'conventional hypothesis', which goes so far as to make econometric predictions of decreases in GDP growth rates due to the single factor of higher oil prices, is not supported by the data for this sample group. This conclusion (as will be noted later) is not contradicted even by the experience of Jamaica, which has an energy-intensive economy which is entirely dependent on imported petroleum.

6.4 Alternative hypotheses

The first oil crisis was interpreted by some analysts as a sudden deflationary shock to all developing countries, regardless of their economic structure. To some extent it is possible to apply this reasoning to certain countries of the sample, and the analysis of Desai in relation to India, Bangladesh, and Sri Lanka, has already been cited.[7] **His analysis concludes that the first oil crisis *irreversibly* impoverished at least Bangladesh, possibly Sri Lanka, and less possibly, India.**

In the case of Bangladesh, the following extract illustrates the analysis developed by Islam, whose text provided the source material for Desai's analysis of Bangladesh.

> We have noted that this increase in crude oil prices was associated with sharp increases in the price of petroleum products and other related commodities. [Elsewhere] we discussed the macro-economic implications of the increase in oil prices. We noted that deteriorations in the terms of trade of Bangladesh were made much worse by the increase [in oil prices]. We also saw that the additional cost of petroleum imports . . . had eaten up the increase in GDP . . .

> The country's capacity to pay for imports also dwindled and this led to a reduction in the volume of imports of some crucial items, including raw materials and capital goods: production in the import-intensive industries suffered heavily.[8]

Islam's assessment of the impact of the first oil crisis on Bangladesh can be traced to a macro-economic analysis of petroleum import price rises, as outlined in the cited text. This analysis is reproduced in its entirety in Table 6.5. In this table, the final row indicates that increased oil prices, plus the higher prices (more or less directly attributable to oil prices) of other imports, were equal to 'a loss of national income' that ranged from 3.53 to 13.45 per cent of GDP, depending on the year. First, however, it is important to note that the data taken directly from Islam's analysis (Table 6.5) do not match the equivalent IBRD data on Bangladesh. In particular, the large fall in GDP, which is shown by Islam as occurring in 1974–5 to 1975–6, is not reflected in IBRD data until the years 1976 and 1977. Yet again, other data, which measure national GDP in constant Bangladeshi currency units, present an entirely different picture of the Bangladeshi economy. Thus, measured in constant Bangladeshi taka, the GDP of Bangladesh is shown to rise consistently throughout the period.

This example is given here to warn of the need for caution in analysing data from different sources, using different base years (for example calendar versus financial), and varying parity rates for the US dollar as against national currencies. The very large variations in Bangladeshi data from different sources make analysis of Bangladesh — using financial data only — an onerous task.

Returning to the analysis by Islam (shown in Table 6.5), it appears that the increased payments for oil (row A) are very large relative to the additional costs of all other imports (row B). However, it must be noted that the 'loss of national income', which according to Islam is between 3.53 to 13.4 per cent per annum, is derived by *adding* row A (oil price rises) to row B (all other import price rises). If row B is removed from the analysis, to give Bangladesh's income loss due to oil price rises alone, the final impact is greatly reduced. For example, the 'loss of income' figure for 1974–5 relative to 1972–3 becomes 2.7 per cent of GDP rather than the 9.12 per cent shown by Islam.

It is of course true that the first oil crisis at least was one of the factors which led to the spread of inflation from country to

Table 6.5 'Some macroeconomic implications of higher oil prices for Bangladesh'

	Factor	*1973–4 over 1972–3*	*1974–5 over 1972–3*	*1975–6 over 1972–3*	*1976–7 over 1972–3*
A	Additional oil costs $US 1 million	39.72	122.72	104.90	121.88
B	Additional costs of other imports due to oil price rises $US 1 million	108.66	427.81	411.07	181.48
C	Additional export earnings due to price rises $US 1 million	14.14	77.35	160.42	190.14
D	GDP at market prices $US billion	6.237	6.037	3.836	3.700
	A as a percentage of D	0.64	2.03	2.73	3.29
	C − B − A $US million	−134.24	−473.18	−355.55	−113.22
E	Actual exports $US 1 million	371.76	382.68	380.47	412.20
	A as a percentage of E	10.7	32.1	27.6	29.6
	A + B as a percentage of E	59.3	143.9	135.6	73.6
	A + B as a percentage of D	3.53	9.12	13.45	8.12

Source: R. Islam, 'Some economic implications of higher oil prices: Bangladesh', ILO Working Paper 52, Geneva, WEPR, November 1979.

country in the OECD from 1978–80. The increase in prices of imported goods from the OECD countries penalised the developing countries, particularly the poorest, such as Bangladesh. Yet it is also true that the first oil crisis triggered off, or aided, a round of price increases for *non-oil* primary products. As can be seen from row C of Table 6.5, even Bangladesh gained from this. For certain countries in the sample, particularly Kenya, Sri Lanka, and Senegal, large but transient gains were made in the period 1972–7 because of substantial increases in the prices for export commodities. However, a repeat of this process in the wake of the second oil crisis is unlikely because of the large decrease in the economic growth of the OECD countries, and because of the world economic recession.

Bangladesh has been — and continues to be — unfortunate in exporting only low-value, substitute, primary and semi-manufactured goods, notably jute. Thus terms of trade for Bangladesh have stayed below parity for 1970 (i.e. 1970=100) throughout the study period. The problem of low prices for Bangladeshi exports appears to be rather more important than the problem of oil import prices, despite the large increases in foreign exchange outflows for oil purchases. To illustrate this, again using data directly from Islam's study, the trends of export and import prices for Bangladesh are compared, and from this comparison is derived the oil-induced depression of commodity terms of trade, as shown in Table 6.6.

Table 6.6 Export and import prices, Bangladesh, 1972-1977

Year	*Export price index*	*Import price index*	*Commodity terms of trade*	
1972–3	100	100	100	
1973–4	105	164	64	
1974–5	127	226	56	
1975–6	178	332	54	
1976–7	213	304	70	Oil-induced depression of commodity terms of trade (per cent)
	Export and import prices indices *excluding* oil			
1972–3	100	100	100	0.0
1973–4	105	160	67	4.5
1974–5	127	213	60	6.7
1975–6	178	313	57	5.2
1976–7	213	277	77	9.0

Source: All data except the final column (author) are taken directly from R. Islam, 'Some economic implications of higher oil prices: Bangladesh'.

It is possible to argue from the analysis shown in Table 6.6 that since the maximum oil component in the erosion of the commodity terms of trade for Bangladesh throughout 1972–7 is 9 per cent, this ratio should be applied in calculating loss of national income. It can be seen from earlier analysis that exports accounted for only 8.6 per cent of GDP in this period (see Table 3.5). If 9 per cent is deducted from this export figure the final result gives a figure of only about 1 per cent, not 13 per cent, for oil-induced loss of GDP. It can be concluded that (excluding the exceptional years of 1976 and 1977, when Bangladesh faced many politico-economic problems, and jute output stagnated) the oil factor appears rather small. The comparison of relative terms of trade movements using Islam's data on Bangladesh (as shown in Table 6.6) shows that the average erosion of terms of trade due to oil was around 5 per cent, excluding 1976–7. It must be asked why, if high oil prices have been such a negative influence (as is maintained by Islam), the oil-induced depression of terms of trade was less for Bangladesh in 1975–6 than in 1976–7. The former year, 1975–6, is claimed by Islam to have been the one in which Bangladesh experienced a 13.45 per cent depression in GDP (relative to 1972–3) due to the price of oil. Thus, both the logic and the supporting data of Islam's study can be challenged. On balance, it appears that Islam's impressive looking claim of a 13 per cent fall in national income 'solely due to high oil prices' is an exaggeration. For Bangladesh, more so than for other countries in this sample, the critical role of weak export prices for a narrow group of primary commodities is the factor which is probably most to blame for the country's constant impoverishment.

6.4.1 Role of petroleum imports in an energy-intensive developing country — the case of Jamaica

It has already been noted that Jamaica has the most energy-intensive economy of all the countries in this sample. In fact Jamaica, which had an energy intensity of 6.60 barrels oil equivalent per $US1,000 of GDP in 1979, is one of the world's most petroleum-intensive economies, and petroleum accounts for about 98 per cent of its commercial energy. Thus, Jamaica presents an extreme example of the significance of the 'petroleum factor' in the adjustment of developing countries.

However, even in this instance it is possible to argue that it was the burden not only of petroleum imports, but also of structural economic and fluctuating terms of trade, that conspired to throw Jamaica to the mercy of the IMF and international creditors. They prescribed deflation, when Jamaica's problems urgently required more dynamic and growth-oriented solutions. The cost of oil imports to Jamaica has been noted by many commentators and analysts, including the Prime Minister of Jamaica, E. Seaga, who commented: 'Jamaica as one of the developing countries is a prime example of how the high cost of energy has adversely affected development. In 1973 Jamaica used the equivalent of 17% of total exports to import oil, while in 1980 the figure was 47%. This has of course created the obvious adverse affects on the economy.'[9]

Jamaica's economy is energy-intensive because 50 per cent of Jamaica's export earnings flow from bauxite and alumina, and the production of alumina from bauxite requires up to 0.5 kilograms of oil (or oil equivalent energy) per kilogram produced. Throughout the period 1973–80 Jamaica used at least 40 per cent of its oil imports, and about 33 per cent of all electricity generated, in the bauxite and alumina industry. Actual data for this period are shown in Table 6.7, together with additional data on the cost of oil imports, and the terms of trade variations for bauxite. The latter indicate that this last factor must be treated as important, rather than ignored completely as in so many analyses of Jamaica's economic problems.

The continuing depression of world alumina and bauxite prices as indicated in Table 6.7, shows to what a small extent the energy content of materials is reflected in their market price. Theoretically, world market prices for such an energy-intensive group of commodities (alumina and bauxite, and finished aluminium) should closely follow oil price movements. This has not happened, for reasons which include production overcapacity in the world aluminium industry,[10] and the trend towards new, more-efficient capacity in the form of cheap hydro- and coal-powered plants located in countries like Sumatra, Indonesia, and Australia. As a result, Jamaica, which is heavily dependent on its aluminium industry, has had to compete in a buyer's market with producers using cheap energy. The lesson from this is that Jamaica suffers from an inappropriate industrial structure, rather than from bad financial management or from problems arising from high oil prices.

6.5 Non-commercial energy

In recent years a number of analysts have reviewed the role of traditional sources of energy, arguing that with 'appropriate management' these sources of energy can entirely or greatly reduce the growth rate of commercial energy demand in the developing countries.[11] Some go much further, and argue that the use of household and non-commercial energy (which is in any case difficult to estimate for most countries) provides a large and real subsidy to the commercial energy system. A recent analysis by the

Table 6.7 Oil use and import costs, and bauxite terms of trade, Jamaica, 1973–1980

Factor	*1973*	*1974*	*1975*	*1976*	*1977*	*1978*	*1979*	*1980*
Oil used in the bauxite and alumina industry (million bfoe)*	10.2	10.7	8.45	6.84	7.49	7.31	7.34	8.23
Oil used in electrical power production † (million bfoe)	2.68	2.49	2.64	2.73	2.79	2.62	2.76	2.68
All other oil uses (million bfoe)	7.13	6.3	6.25	6.15	5.92	6.58	6.16	4.25
Cost of oil imports ($Jam. millions)	71.5	195	209	200	220	216	331	451
Terms of trade for bauxite (1968=100)	66	98	94	99	104	98	91	92

* bfoe — barrels fuel oil equivalent.

† In 1980, for example, about 34 per cent of total electrical power was used directly by the bauxite and alumina industries — see Jamaican Petroleum Corporation, *National Energy Outlook*, Kingston, JPC, October 1981.

Sources: For oil use and oil import costs see JPC, *National Energy Outlook*, October 1979. For bauxite trade terms see IBRD, *Commodity Trade and Price Trends*, Washington DC, IBRD, August 1981.

Commonwealth Institute in London illustrates this approach. The study comments:

> Compared with the usually presented picture . . . developing countries' consumption of [all] energy is greater in total [when household and non-commercial energy is added]. A broad estimate is of at least 1.5 billion tons coal equivalent, compared with 0.9 billion tons for commercial fuels alone, and in per capita terms at least 720 kgs coal equivalent in 1978 compared with 450 kgs for commercial fuels. [As a result] their proportion of global consumption is higher, at least 16% in 1978 compared with 11% [on the basis of commercial fuels alone].[12]

By utilising this form of argument, and choosing certain 'conversion factors' for the commercial energy equivalence of household and non-commercial energy fuels as energy subsidisers to the modern sector, a whole range of theories can be developed, notably on the real energy intensities of the economies of developing countries. It is possible (but no indication of data bases is given from which a definitive conclusion can be drawn) that the data in the IBRD *World Development Report*of 1981 incorporate an estimate of the additional 'energy subsidy' to GDP from household and non-commercial energy in 1980. The author's calcuations for this study indicate that a figure much closer to 3.2 to 3.5 boe per $US1,000 of GDP would more accurately represent the household and non-commercial energy 'subsidy' in developing countries.

The efficiency of agriculture utilising household and non-commercial energy compared with that of farming systems which are commercial energy intensive has been studied for many regions of the world. The data shown in Table 6.8 compare Indian farming with that of the OECD countries. It is evident from these data that to raise output, even in the relatively capital-extensive agricultural sector (which has about one-fifth to one-tenth the capital investment per worker relative to most industry),[13] demands extra commercial energy. Thus the existence of high levels of household and non-commercial energy dependence in the rural areas of developing countries (estimated by some analysts to be about 90 per cent of total energy needs for 90 per cent of the rural population)[14] can be called a direct check on accumulation and development. All the sample countries in this study, especially the four low-income countries, confirm this low-energy/low-output problem in rural

Table 6.8 Index of output per worker and energy intensity of inputs in agriculture, India and certain OECD countries, 1970–1975 (India = 100)

Country	*India*	*Italy*	*France*	*Federal Republic of Germany*	*USA*
Output per worker	100	520	567	553	1,317
Energy input per unit of output	100	670	1,250	2,500	3,330

Source:
A. Desai, *Development and Energy Consumption*, Delhi, International Energy Studies, John Wiley, 1980.

areas. This is easily verified from the data shown in Tables 5.4 and 5.5, which indicate that rural workers produce only about one-third to one-fifth of the output of industrial workers.

Further, it is likely that the actual process of development depends on the stability and growth of commercial energy, which was shown to be absent in many of the sample countries. The dependence of the sample countries on primary product exports was very marked and subjected them to sharp swings in demand, with immediate repercussions on commercial energy demand. The pattern of unstable, rapidly changing, and variable commercial energy demand prevents or slows the development of more organised and integrated energy networks.

It is important to note that household and non-commercial energy cannot easily act as a substitute for modern commercial energy. This can be illustrated through reference to the 'firewood crisis' of many developing countries. The problem exists in at least three of the sample countries, and is critical in Senegal,[15] very serious in Bangladesh,[16] and increasing in Kenya.[17] In recent years[18] the solution offered to the problems of land loss, desertification, resource waste, and diffusion of human effort (largely attributable to a pre-industrial dependence on biomass energy in the developing countries) has featured proposals for huge firewood plantations. Advocates of such programmes have been careful to depict the alternative as a sombre vision of approaching cataclysms (social, political, economic, and environmental) in the rural areas of developing countries.[19]

Essentially, the rationale of such smartly tailored 'crisis mentality' contains a serious error in logic. This is that the firewood crisis (caused primarily by over-rapid use of wood) can be solved through increasing the use of wood as an energy source. Further, the philosophy of these advocates of a 'solar tomorrow' is that the rural areas, at least, of developing countries should **forget the 'cul-de-sac' of modern development.[20] The basic** causes of the firewood shortage in rural and urban areas of developing countries can be stated as:

(i) strong demographic pressure on resource bases;
(ii) decreasing per capita household and non-commercial energy resources due to (i) above, to erosion/desertification, and to changes in land use; and
(iii) little or no regulation or organisation of resource bases, **notably replanting and protection, etc.**

One simple cause of all these problems, and undoubtedly the dominant one, is the fact of poverty. This continuing problem interacts negatively with any tendencies for spontaneous change, such as the growth of more stable, larger fuel markets vertically integrated to include resource management. In fact, household and non-commercial energy fuel production, marketing (where this exists), and use is essentially pre-industrial. Only by improving the product, notably by energy densification and increased efficiency of use, can non-commercial energy fuels (for example wood, crop residues, biogas, etc.) command markets. Only then will a parallel energy system be able to compete with conventional commercial energy (oil, gas, and electricity). The reason this has not occurred is simple: a vicious circle of poverty prevents the required capital investment. This perspective on the problem of rural energy supplies in developing countries is often missing in the sometimes unrealistic 'debate' on the use of new and renewable energy sources in such countries.[21]

Household and non-commercial energy will of course continue to play a major role in developing countries, particularly in rural areas. However, the extreme inefficiency of use (rarely 10 per cent), the great waste of plant, soil, and human resources, and the problems of substituting household and non-commercial energy for commercial energy indicate that increased human output, requiring more commercial energy, remains the short- to medium-term priority in development. Only when income levels are substantially raised can there be realistic prospects for the widespread use of improved household and non-commercial energy (and more unconventional) sources in the developing countries.

6.6 Capital investment in the energy sector

For decades, the IBRD and other institutions have strongly favoured the development of oil-fired electrical power systems in developing countries.[22] While these often gave very good returns on investment, they are now open to criticism on the grounds that they left the developing countries particularly vulnerable to oil-related adjustment problems through the absence of more balanced, indigenous commercial energy systems.

Since 1975–9, following repeated criticisms of the gap in the development of the energy sector, many proposals have emerged,[23] and the IBRD itself has proposed increasingly larger oil, coal, and gas development programmes for the developing countries. Despite this, energy sector investment analysis by the IBRD still heavily favours electrical power. A recent projection by the IBRD, shown in Table 6.9, illustrates this. The gigantic sums shown in this table need only be compared with the UNIDO data shown in Table 4.1, which assume a grant total for capital investment of all

Table 6.9 Electrical power and other energy investment projections for all developing countries, 1981–1990 (1980 $US)

Electrical power source	*MW installed*	*Cost ($ billions)*
Thermal	144,100	167
Hydro	101,700	176
Nuclear	34,700	67
Geothermal	1,900	4
Total	282,400	414
All energy investments		550–1,000

Source: IBRD, *Energy in Developing Countries,* Washington DC, IBRD, 1980; the final row is the author's estimate.

kinds (plant and infrastructure) in all oil-importing developing countries of about $US1,375 billion (at 1977 prices) or about $US1,895 billion (at 1980 prices). The sums shown in Table 6.9 can be reduced by no more than about 30 per cent to exclude oil-exporting developing countries' power system development, leaving around $US290 billion (at 1980 prices) as the power system needs of the remaining developing countries. Dividing this between poorer and middle-income developing countries according to the UNIDO ratio for all investment results in the respective (and approximate) allocations shown in Table 6.10

Although the figures in Table 6.10 are by their very nature imprecise, and have been radically changed during the period 1979–81 by the IBRD itself, it is useful to look at their implications for the sample countries. Thus Table 6.11 shows the energy sector capital investment implications of the IBRD and UNIDO projections, based on income-group, for the sample countries. These energy sector capital investment implications are then compared in Table 6.12 with the 1979 Gross Domestic Investment (as shown in Table 5.6) of the sample countries. It must be stressed that these

Table 6.10 Division of energy sector capital investment between all developing countries, by income group, 1981–1990 (1980 $US billions)

Sector	*Developing country income group* Lower-income	Middle-income	Total
Electrical power	66	230	290
All other energy	22–59	118–315	150–400

Source: Author's estimates, based on data from the IBRD, UNIDO, and others.

Table 6.11 Approximate commercial energy sector capital investment needs relative to finance gaps, for each of the sample countries 1981–1990 (1980 $US billions)

Country and income group		*Income group's share of total 1979 population (per cent)*	*Approximate energy sector needs ($US billions)* Electrical power	Other
Poorer developing countries	Bangladesh	4.5	3.0	1.0–2.6
	Sri Lanka	0.66	0.5	0.16–0.42
Middle-income developing countries	Kenya	2.3	5.3	2.7–7.3
	Senegal	0.85	1.9	1.0–2.6
	Peru	2.6	6.0	3.1–8.2
	Jamaica	0.33	0.8	0.4–1.1

Source: Author's calculations, based on the IBRD and UNIDO projections cited in Section 6.6.

Table 6.12 Gross Domestic Investment (GDI) and commercial energy sector capital investment projections for each of the sample countries in the 1980s

Country	*GDI 1973–9 (1980 $US millions)*	*Energy sector investment (1980 $US billions)* Electrical power	Other	*Ratio of energy sector needs to GDI*
Bangladesh	745	3.0	1.0–2.6	5.4–7.5
Sri Lanka	585	0.5	0.16–0.42	1.1–7.5
Kenya	1,215	5.3	2.7–7.3	6.6–10.3
Senegal	485	1.9	1.0–2.6	6.0–9.3
Peru	2,455	6.0	3.1–8.2	3.7–5.8
Jamaica	435	0.8	0.4–1.1	2.8–4.4

Source: Author's calculations, based on the IBRD and UNIDO projections cited in Section 6.6.

figures are estimates, incorporating great uncertainties, and it must also be assumed that aggregated figures from UNIDO and the IBRD can be disaggregated on a population and income-group basis. However, the figures in Tables 6.11 and 6.12 do suggest that energy investment projections for the developing countries are vast. The final column in table 6.12 can be read as the number of years of each country's average GDP needed to satisfy the energy sector requirements alone from 1981–90. Only the figure for Sri Lanka is remotely acceptable, when allowance is made for non-energy investment needs. These figures add another dimension to the analyses in Chapters 4 and 5, especially if it is (quite reasonably) assumed that non-electrical power investments should at least equal those in the electricity sector.

Notes

1. The 'Big-Eight' of Brazil, South Korea, Taiwan, India, Turkey, Thailand, Cuba, and the Philippines imported 139.5 million tons of oil in 1979. Total imports for the OECD countries in the same year were 293 million tons. See Economic Intelligence Unit, *Oil Imports of Developing Countries — Forecasts to 1995*, Report 125, London, EIU, July 1982.
2. See, for example, sections relating to energy in developing countries in and IEA, *World Energy Outlook*, Paris, IEA, 1982.
3. See for example, sections relating to energy in developing countries in IBRD, *World Development Report*, New York, Oxford University Press, 1980, 1981; UNESCAP, *Short-term Economic Policy Aspects of the Energy Situation in the ESCAP Region*, Bangkok, UNESCAP, 1981; and Commonwealth Institute, *The World Economic Crisis*, Economic Paper 13, London, Commonwealth Secretariat, September 1980.
4. J. Katz and O. Marwah, *Nuclear Power in Developing Countries*, Washington DC, Lexington Books, 1982.
5. IBRD, *Energy in the Developing Countries*, Washington DC, IBRD, August 1980.
6. IBRD, *World Development Report*, 1981, Chapters 4 and 5.
7. M. Desai, 'Effects of the rise in oil prices on South Asian countries, 1972–8, *ILO Review*, 120/2, March–April 1981.
8. R. Islam, 'Some economic implictions of higher oil prices: Bangladesh', ILO Working Paper 52, Geneva, WEPR, November 1979.
9. Introductory message in Ministry of Mining and Energy, *Jamaica National Energy Plan*, Kingston, 1981.
10. *Financial Times*, London, 18 February 1981.
11. See, for example, UNIDO, *Appropriate Industrial Technologies for Energy for Rural Requirements*, Vienna, UNIDO, 1979.

12. Commonwealth Institute, op. cit.
13. See, for example, B. Herman, *The Optimal International Division of Labour*, Geneva, ILO, 1975.
14. M. Chatterji, *Energy and Environment in Developing Countries*, Chichester, John Wiley, 1981.
15. Commission of the European Community, 'Dossier-désertification', *EEC-ACP Courier*, **47**, 1978.
16. Katz nd Marwah, op. cit.
17. Commission of the European Community, op. cit.
18. Notably at the UN Conference on New and Renewable Sources of Energy, Nairobi, August-September 1981.
19. E.g. E. Eckholm, *Forestry for Human Needs*, Paper 26, Washington DC, Worldwatch Institute, February 1976.
20. E.g. D. Hayes, *Perspectives on Solar Energy*, Paper 15, Washington DC, Worldwatch Institute, 1977.
21. E.g. *Synthesis Report*, 100/PC/41, New York, UN, March 1981.
22. See, for example, A. MacKillop, 'Energy for the developing world', *Energy Policy*, December 1980.
23. See, for example, IBRD, *Minerals and Energy in Developing Countries*, Report 1588, Washington DC, IBRD, May 1977.

7 PERSPECTIVES ON THE ENERGY ISSUE IN DEVELOPING COUNTRIES

7.1 Introduction

Since the time of the first oil crisis, and more so since the second, the energy issue has become magnified out of all proportion. Because of the large demand for transport fuel in many developing countries, liquid petroleum fuel substitutes are usually given priority for technical development. There are some substitutes for petroleum, notably alcohol fuel, which are technically feasible but whose economic limitations are now being recognised.

Since the late 1970s many proposals for an increased use of unconventional new and renewable energy sources (NRSE) have been advocated, often as key to 'energy transition' in the developing countries. Only three of the sample countries have extensive programmes in the NRSE sector, and one of these has already experienced significant economic difficulties with these 'alternatives'. For numerous reasons, it is suggested in this chapter that NRSE are not currently economical for developing countries, with certain specific exceptions.

7.1.1 Liquid fuels and substitutes

The role of liquid petroleum in the transport sector can be substituted, but only with real economic (but not technical) difficulty. This is simply because production vehicles are designed to use gasolene, diesel fuel, or liquid petroleum gas. The use of an ethanol alternative, which attracted much attention at the time of its introduction — it was labelled the 'best bet' for virtually all developing countries with agricultural potential — has proved, at the least, questionable. One of the most striking facts is that the energy output required to produce ethanol fuel is much higher than the energy yielded from it. Apart from this, there are many other problems associated with it, relating notably to the environmental impacts of wastes and the high cost of 'reprocessing' should this option be pursued.

All the sample countries (except Jamaica) show a high usage of petroleum, relative to total energy sources, in their transport sectors, as is shown in Table 7.1. In Jamaica, where the alumina and bauxite industry dominates oil use, the share of the transport sector is quite low. The share is large for Bangladesh, given the country's very low road density — about 100 miles per 1,000 square kilometres in the 1970s, compared to similar figures of 370 miles for India and 480 miles for Sri Lanka in the same period. Conversely, the share is relatively low for Kenya, though the transport sector is showing high growth. Other developing countries have comparable ranges — in 1978 the transport sector consumed 54.1 per cent of all oil products in Pakistan, 43.1 per cent in Thailand, and 56.5 per cent in Brazil.

Table 7.1 Total petroleum consumption and transport share for each of the sample countries, dates indicated

Country	*Total petroleum use (tons x 1,000)*	*Transport use (tons x 1,000)*	*Transport use as a percentage of total use*	*Total oil use per capita (kilograms)*
Bangladesh 1974	907	204	22.6	11.5
Sri Lanka 1978	1,062	624	58.7	74.0
Kenya 1979	2,739	569	20.8	170.0
Senegal 1975	807	242	30.0	150.0
Peru 1976	6,080	2,550	41.9	380.0
Jamaica 1979	2,320	340	14.7	1,050.0

Sources: Bangladesh and Sri Lanka — IBRD, *World Development Report*, New York, Oxford University Press, 1981; Kenya — UNDP/IBRD, *Kenya — Issues and Options in the Energy Sector*, Report 3800-KE, New York, IBRD, 1981; Senegal — NRSE, *A Case Study of Senegal*, Oxford, NRSE, CENRENIEO, 1981; Peru — 'A case study of Peru', in M. Chatterji, *Energy and Environment in Developing Countries*, Chichester, John Wiley, 1981.

Broadly speaking, the conventional solutions to this problem centre around alternatives in fuel or refinery practices. The latter have been featured in several IBRD publications on this subject, but they are very costly. Changing refinery installations to give a higher output of lighter products for transport can add 40 per cent to capital costs. The alternative fuel options featured, for a while, the biomass fuels — mainly ethanol, since methanol is essentially untried, and extremely toxic. After an initial 'guarded optimism' the IBRD has changed its views on this so-called 'alternative', as is shown by the IBRD *World Development Report* of 1980. The UNDP/IBRD report on Kenya made the following comments about the advisability of Kenya continuing with its very high-cost ethanol fuel programme:

> The mission concluded that the [Kenyan] Government had not dealt systematically with the economic, technical, organisational and financial issues relating to the introduction of fuel alcohol . . . including high capital costs, transport costs for molasses, external energy costs . . . the profitable molasses export markets, and above all the fact that gasoline landed at Mombasa at US$ 1.10/ US gal. still has a highly competitive price relative to [alcohol] . . .
>
> The mission therefore recommends first that no further investments be made in the fuel alcohol program.[1]

It is useful to note that a price of $US1.10 per 3.785 litres (one US gallon) is over $US46 per barrel, while market crudes (after allowing for numerous price discounts, delayed payment arrangements, etc.) have a current (1982–3) real price of around $US27–32 per barrel. More than ever, this kind of U-turn on the policy and support for 'alternative' fuels shows the reality of the situation, which is that:

(i) the most energy- and resource-efficient transport is composed of fixed route, high-mass systems (rail and water);
(ii) the near-term substitute for petroleum is petroleum, either imported or indigenous; and
(iii) a more-balanced liquid fuels demand structure requires overall economic development.

Unfortunately, it is taking time for this reality to be recognised. As a consequence, economically and technically unrealistic proposals, particularly for NRSE programmes in developing countries, have been popularised although they ignore the economic reality of these countries.[2] The preceding extract from the UNDP/IBRD report[3] should be compared with IBRD pronouncements of the recent past which, conversely, have favoured the use of alcohol fuel in developing countries. That such changes in viewpoint can occur so rapidly illustrates a point constantly reiterated in this study: policy can never be dissociated from an analysis of underlying economic structures and trends. When it is — as in the drive for alternative energy — it can produce costly and embarrassing mistakes.

The fact that developing countries in general tend to use 30 to 50 per cent of their liquid fuel (all of which may be imported) for transport is yet another indication of the immaturity of their infrastructures. As these develop, both in the industrial and the transport sector, a downward pressure on the proportion of liquid fuel used in transport will operate from two directions, namely: *(a)* the emergence of non-transport liquid fuel uses (offering better-balanced fuel mixes) and *(b)* the development of more capital-intensive, better-organised fixed route high-mass transport modes. The fact that such modes were developed before the advent of gasolene/diesel road transport in the industrial countries (where liquid fuel accounts for only about 20 to 35 per cent of total petroleum use) is due to historical coincidence, that is, the absence of this much lower capital-cost alternative at the time of the Industrial Revolution.

Proposals for alternative refinery structures in the developing countries (namely, the use of various 'cracker' technologies) demand very great additional investment. Further, the world surplus of oil-refining capacity (which may last as long as ten years) offers better short-term prospects for developing countries by enabling them to operate policies based on economic principles. Such policies would aim at satisfying middle- and heavier-product demand with supplies from home refineries, and importing the balance. Nevertheless, it is obvious that industrial development will increase the demand for fuel oil, and therefore it is possible that many developing countries will eventually develop least-cost refinery practices, rather than attempt the reverse.

7.2 Alternative energy in the sample countries

It will be recalled that Jamaica has the most energy-intensive economy in this sample, with the most capital-intensive economic infrastructure. In the days of cheap oil it was much more rational than it is today to develop the world's most energy-intensive primary ore-refining industry (bauxite to alumina) in an energy-poor country.

7.2.1 Jamaica — energy programme and policy

The political impact of higher oil prices is recognised by Jamaica, as is frequently indicated by Jamaican politicians in their statements on this subject. The *Jamaica National Energy Plan*[4] lists the following as major priorities:

(i) diversification of petroleum sources;
(ii) delivery and widespread use of appropriate NRSE;
(iii) exploration for oil, gas, and geothermal energy; and
(iv) an energy stockpile (oil).

The plan divides energy development into time phases of one to five and five to ten years, and over ten years, and then goes on to identify conservation potentials for the near and medium term. The NRSE considered to be useful within the three time phases are:

Near term (one to five years) — solar water heaters; small- and medium-scale hydropower research and development effort on ethanol fuel.

Medium term (five to ten years) — power generation from garbage if economic; large-scale hydropower; biogas on a small scale; other biogas; more solar water heating; development and use of solar thermal power generation.

Long term (over ten years) — ocean thermal energy; solar pond electricity; high-temperature solar thermal electricity; wood-fired power plants; waste burning.

Bearing in mind that around 50 per cent of all Jamaica's oil imports are used in refining bauxite to alumina, it is significant that energy conservation in this sector is *not* emphasised. Using the forecasts and data of the Jamaica Bauxite Institute Ltd., the specific consumption of energy per ton of alumina produced is projected to fall by only 2.5 per cent from 1977–85.[5] By comparison, official Japanese projections of energy use in alumina refining estimate a 21 per cent reduction in specific energy use over the same period.[6]

Of the NRSE featured earlier, only hydropower plants are technically and economically competitive with other power sources based on fuels (notably coal, which is featured in the Jamaican plan as an oil substitute). Moreover, most imported solar water-heating systems appear economically viable only in comparison with electric water heating. This indicates that in this sector other potential sources which are technically viable could fruitfully be examined. It should be noted that Jamaica's population is 50 per cent urban and increasing at twice the country's population growth rate. Therefore, heat recovery systems based on individual total energy systems are particularly good for Jamaica[7] because they supply both electricity and heat for air conditioning and water heating in building blocks, offices, and other commercial premises.

Of the other alternative sources listed earlier, biogas — while technically and economically feasible in certain conditions[8] — has a limited potential. The remainder are essentially uneconomic, technically unproved, or both. Of course, this does not mean that these sectors are totally without potential but, rather, that the time horizons of Jamaica's energy plans are not long enough to allow for the technical and economic maturity of many of these systems.

While programmes such as the replacement of oil-fired power generation by coal are clearly economic (even allowing for about 20 per cent additional capital costs for coal as against oil), coal is still about 70 to 90 per cent cheaper than oil,[9] the bulk of Jamaican NRSE potentials are quite costly. Furthermore, they are of a very small scale. Using the estimates given,[10] the maximum potential of all non-hydropowered NRSE in the period 1980–90 amounts to 253,600 barrels fuel oil equivalent per annum. This is equal to about 1.6 per cent of Jamaica's oil consumption in 1980.

Clearly, Jamaica is faced with tough energy choices. Its present economic structure is very energy-intensive, and extremely narrowly-based. Thus, rather than examining the energy sector alone and looking for solutions which do not exist, attention must turn to the broader energy-economic picture. Here it is notable that other Caribbean countries, specialising to a greater extent in commerce, offshore industry, services, counter-season agriculture, and so on, have often adjusted more successfully than Jamaica. This does not offer an immediate solution to the problem but it does reinforce the argument that economic adjustment cannot be found in changes in the energy sector alone. This is as true for Jamaica, the most energy-intensive of the sample countries, as it is for Bangladesh.

7.2.2 Kenya — from alternatives to conservation

It has already been noted (Section 7.1.1) that the IBRD, in company with the UNDP, now believe that Kenya is mistaken in pursuing its ethanol fuel programme. However, this change in attitude came about only *after* Kenya had set up a programme whose estimated cost is about $US20 million and which was due to start production in 1982.[11] It is interesting to compare the IBRD's present attitude with its views in 1980 when Kenya was one of two *named* countries, outside of Brazil, where the manufacture of ethanol fuel from molasses was considered 'attractive' by the IBRD, at least in theory.[12]

The UNDP/IBRD report of 1981[13] has concentrated for the most part on recommendations relating to the conservation and rationalisation of energy use, with only small — but quite significant — attention being paid to NRSE. Thus, their approach is now quite similar to that advocated by CENRENIEO,[14] and recommends:

(i) an increase in the supply of energy;
(ii) rationalisation of the use of imported petroleum;
(iii) development of indigenous energy resources; and
(iv) reduced dependence on imported oil.

As has been shown in Chapters 3 and 5, the export price structure of Kenya's predominantly agricultural output, its narrow industrial and manufacturing sector, and its energy demand performance over the period 1970–9 all suggest an instability typical of the sample countries. This has had a direct impact on the energy sector. Thus, the UNDP/IBRD report discusses oil imports, refineries, oil products trade, and related questions in detail. The report notes the faster growth in domestic demand for light products (transport and domestic kerosenes) relative to heavy products, and also notes that similar patterns can be seen in the oil markets dependent on Kenyan exports (Kenya's refinery at Mombasa sends refined products to Rwanda, Burundi, and Uganda). The report therefore concludes that the Kenyan refinery is producing too much of the heavier products, for example fuel oil, and not enough gasolene, kerosene, and diesel fuel. This is virtually a world-wide problem, which results in surplus shipments of heavy products chasing fewer and fewer customers. Conversely, the price of lighter products is firm because of increased demand.

Thus the Kenyan refinery operation, which until 1973 covered the cost of almost *all* oil imports through the profits made on sales to dependent markets, is now seriously in deficit. The UNDP/IBRD report suggests a number of responses, and on the technical level these feature the installation of the cheapest type of cracker, at a cost of about $US85 million, in order to increase light products in proportion to total output.[15] Where the report shows the structure of output, relative to changes in demand since 1973, the large fall in demand for heavy boiler fuel stands out. The product distribution trends since 1973 are reproduced in Table 7.2 and Figure 7.1. Since the category 'heavy fuel oil and industrial diesel' is the fuel most used by industry, the fall in demand for this product strongly reinforces the observations made in Chapters 3, 5, and 6. That is to say, the increased variability of terms of trade, heavier debt, increasing population pressure, and other factors have greatly slowed real development, in the sense of broadening the economic base. At the same time, the acute shortage of fuel wood in many rural areas of Kenya, plus some increase in rural incomes, has stimulated demand for kerosene (the obvious substitute for fuel wood) and transport fuels. In the light of these observations it is easy to query the thesis that the oil problems in Kenya are attributable to a structural problem of demand, and to advance the view that, rather, they are the result of slowed, de-stabilised national economic development.

It is notable how a new 'realism' permeates the UNDP/IBRD report in the sections relating to NRSE. Conservation of energy is advocated on the basis of rather dubious observations made by

Table 7.2 Ratio of growth in petroleum product demand to growth in GDP in Kenya, 1969–80

Product	*1969–73*	*1973–80*
Liquid petroleum gas	3.06	1.85
Gasoline	1.69	0.79
Kerosene	0.88	1.53
Jet fuel	2.14	0.96
Gas oil	2.05	1.49
Heavy diesel	1.62	−0.79
Fuel oil	0.82	0.36
Aviation spirit	−0.06	0.06
Total	1.54	0.87

Source: UNDP/IBRD, *Kenya — Issues and Options in the Energy Sector.*

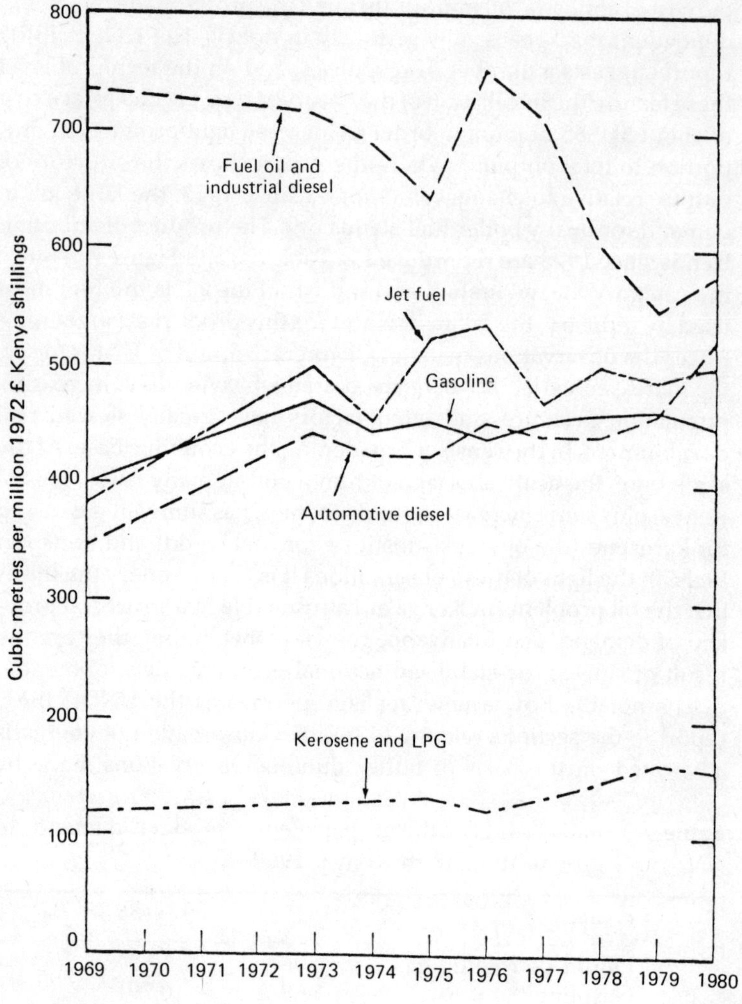

Fig. 7.1 Petroleum product consumption related to GDP in Kenya 1969–1980

visiting experts,[16] who claim that energy use 'per unit of output in the industrial sector . . . could be reduced by 20%–30% over the next 5 years without substantial new capital investment'. Yet this goal is supposed to be attainable *before* the establishment of a detailed data base on industrial and commercial energy use!

Of the NRSE, it is solar water heating that currently claims the report's attention. Significantly, the use of this system is claimed to be applicable only to the luxury housing sector as a replacement for electric water heating, which at present uses around 4 per cent of total commercial energy. The Kenyan electricity authorities have already introduced off-peak water heating tariffs, with the aim of stabilising power demand at night and throughout weekends when — as in many developing countries[17] — electricity demand plummets. Thus solar water heating cannot simply be weighed against power costs and marginal savings, but must take account of the capacity of electricity-generating plants — a point often ignored in debating this NRSE. In addition, the fact that all solar water heaters are imported, and are taxed accordingly, makes them luxury items. It is significant that this problem is rarely touched upon in the report, whereas that of power demand management is widely discussed even though the maximum credible savings from any level of solar heating installation are very low.

The report mentions certain other NRSE, such as wind power and biogas, but these are of very little significance compared to the actual potential of hydropower and the large possibilities in the geothermal energy sector. The report notes that from 1957–78 the total expenditure on oil exploration amounted to only 12 million Kenyan shillings, while the ethanol fuel adventure is costing at least 35 million Kenyan shillings for a yield of indisputably uneconomic fuels. This must rank as a major (but unstated) failing of much recent European and American energy aid and counselling to the developing countries.

It is significant that Kenya has good economic growth prospects. However, it now also has an energy problem. This is not simply a problem of over-rapid growth, of a retreat from household and non-commercial energy use (the UNDP/IBRD report suggests of course that this energy source can be stabilised), or of high oil import prices. In fact, like the other three agricultural primary product exporters in the sample, Kenya has experienced tremendous instability in the external markets for its narrow range of export goods, concurrent with rapid urbanisation and the maintenance of at least a small (1.5 to 2.5 per cent per annum) per capita increase in income. Thus the secular and social changes (urbanisation, better education, etc.) have increased demand for commercial energy fuels and transport, while the unstable economic structure has at the same time presented sustained growth of industry. This pattern cannot be maintained for long, here or in other developing countries, before it results in the negative sequences noted in Chapters 3-5 and elsewhere. Tinkering with experimental, costly, or inappropriate NRSE, and, to some extent, with conservation also, is literally addressing non-problems (or small ones) while letting the larger ones get out of control. As the OECD countries, the newly industrialising countries, and some developing countries have shown, growth and development with adjustment is a far more successful policy than recklessly throwing resources into the energy sector.

Thus in Sri Lanka there exists a rural energy centre, funded principally by UNCRET, UNDP, and others.[18] This concentrates several NRSE in one centre, where they can be effectively analysed and monitored. All but hydropowered NRSE are treated as longer-term possibilities. In Senegal, a number of Franco–Senegalese projects centred on solar heat and solar electricity technologies have been established.[19] These allow European organisations to gain useful field experience in rugged user-environments and the host country to gain, at low cost and commitment, working examples of new technologies.

Notes

1. UNDP/IBRD, *Kenya — Issues and Options in the Energy Sector*, Report 3800-KE, New York, IBRD, 1981.
2. See, for example, A. MacKillop, :Energy in the developing world', *International Journal of Energy Research*, March 1981.
3. UNDP/IBRD, op. cit.
4. Ministry of Mining and Energy, *Jamaica National Energy Plan*, Kingston, 1981.
5. Jamaica Bauxite Institute Ltd., *Annual Report*, Kingston, JBI, 1981.
6. T. Toichi, *State and Future Potentials of Energy Conservation in Japan*, Tokyo, Institute of Energy Economics, 1979.
7. A. MacKillop, 'Unconventional energy: costs performance and employment implications in developing countries', Geneva, ILO, forthcoming.
8. Ibid.

9. Notably IBRD, *World Development Report*, New York, Oxford University Press, 1981, Chapters 4 and 5.
10. Ministery of Mining and Energy, op. cit.
11. UNDP/IBRD, op. cit.
12. IBRD, *World Development Report*, 1980.
13. UNDP/IBRD, op. cit.
14. NRSE, *A Case Study of Kenya*, Oxford, NRSE, CENRENIEO, 1981.
15. UNDP/IBRD, op. cit.
16. E.g. L. Schipper *et al.*, *Measuring Energy Conservation in Kenya*, Paper 12741, Cal., Lawrence Berkeley Laboratory, 1981.
17. M. Munasingha, *Economics of Power Systems, Reliability and Planning*, Baltimore, Johns Hopkins University Press, 1979.
18. See, for example, I.H. Usmani, *Power to the Villages*, Mazingira, UNEP/ Pergamon Press, 1978.
19. NRSE, *A Case Study of Senegal*, Oxford, NRSE, CENRENIEO, 1981.

8 SUMMARY OF CONCLUSIONS

8.1 The subject matter of this book has engendered heated debate in international fora and academic institutions, and between the politicians and economists of the OECD and Third World countries. In spite of the fact that the analysis and data presented in this study and the turn of events since 1973 prove many of the points advanced by Third World countries about the development of the global economy, the debate will no doubt continue.

8.2 Since 1945, the two major institutions to lay down the rules of economic and development behaviour have been the IBRD and the IMF. Between 1973 and 1980 these two institutions evolved new sets of criteria for 'adjustment' to the sharp rises in oil prices after 1973. Although these criteria are of a global nature, their cumulative impact on developing countries has been extremely negative.

8.3 This study has examined the impact of the rise in oil prices in conjunction with the monetarist policies of the United States and major European countries on a sample of six developing countries.

8.4 The countries chosen for this study represent but a small fraction of the world's oil importers (below 0.25 per cent), and have a very small aggregate GDP. An analysis of the performance of their economies from 1970–9 reveals a number of characteristics. As regards industrial growth in this period, only Sri Lanka showed signs of noted growth. Kenya, Bangladesh, and Senegal showed particularly low rates of growth. All six of the countries in the sample showed a higher dependence on primary product exports in 1978–9 relative to the 1950–70 average for countries with similar GNP per capita. This was particularly marked in the cases of Sri Lanka, Senegal, Peru and Jamaica. Sri Lanka and Kenya showed growth in Gross Domestic Investment (measured as a share of GDP) relative to the 1950–70 average for their similar-income group of countries. Investment was particularly low in Peru, Jamaica, and Bangladesh.

In only one country — Kenya — did the GDP per capita growth rate average over 2 per cent per annum during 1970–8. Senegal, Bangladesh, Jamaica, and Peru showed a decline in GDP per capita in the same period. In the cases of Senegal and Jamaica, this decline was due to a contraction in the overall economies of these countries.

8.5 As regards trade and terms of trade, there were noticeable trends during 1972–80. The period 1972–5 was one of rapid negative change following the first increase in oil prices. The period 1975–7 showed an improvement in trade deficits, and two of the six sample countries showed surpluses. During 1977–80, the countries which had gained on primary commodity terms of trade experienced a sudden reversal, with rising deficits. Senegal and Bangladesh were worst hit. However, in the long-run period 1968–79, measured in constant currency terms, all the sample countries showed annual import growth rates well above export growth rates. In the first adjustment period of 1972–6 only Kenya showed surpluses in its terms of trade.

8.6 Throughout the study period all the oil-importing countries of the sample experienced large increases in current account deficits as a percentage of GDP. The only exceptions were Sri Lanka and Kenya, which recorded current account surpluses after the recovery in non-oil commodity terms of trade. After the first increase in oil prices (1973–4) there was a brief recovery period (1973–6), except for Peru and Jamaica. The other four countries showed drastic reductions in their current account deficits. This reversal of trends is explained by improved commodity prices, by financial flows (in the form of aid and grants) into these countries, and by the brief recovery in the OECD countries at this time.

After 1977–9, the cumulative impact of rising national debt costs, stagnant or falling commodity prices, and falling growth rates in the OECD countries, followed by the second rise in oil prices, combined to increase once more current account deficits as a percentage of GNP. This pattern did not occur in the special cases of Peru (by then an oil exporter) and Jamaica (because of the continued contraction of its economy).

8.7 Significantly, apart from Bangladesh all of the sample countries showed lower annual growth rates of national debt and inflation in the period 1973–9 than in the period 1970–9. However, the growth of real public debt was very high at between 3 and 15 times the rate of economic growth. Debt costs for most countries (except Bangladesh and Sri Lanka) showed continuous growth rates, reflected in the annual interest payment transfers abroad, which increased as rapidly, or more rapidly, than GNP or national debt. The evidence of this study is that there was a good correlation between growth of national debt and GNP per capita (apart from Bangladesh). At the beginning of the study period there was no close relationship between GNP per capita and the measure of debt service as a percentage of GNP. At the end of the period this relationship is shown to be very significant. The higher-income developing countries in particular, and all the sample countries (except, perhaps, Sri Lanka) face the 1980s with very heavy debt burdens.

8.8 The generally low commercial energy consumption per capita, and its low growth rate, were apparent in the sample countries. Each country's growth rate in the consumption of commercial energy was compared with that for all developing countries (as a group) for certain years. The commercial energy trends in the sample countries were found to show the following:

(i) Volatility There were very large percentage variations in the sample countries' commercial energy trends, especially when compared with those for all developing countries. For all countries except Jamaica this volatility was much greater after 1973.

(ii) Energy-economic intensities All countries except Jamaica showed high energy efficiency (low commercial energy input per unit of GNP output). A declining trend of energy efficiency, due at least partly to urbanisation and industrialisation, is evident in the longer-run (1970–80) trends. Energy intensification of the economy was particularly marked in Peru, Senegal, and Bangladesh. The role of terms of trade and GDP movement is evident in the sudden reversals of this intensification trend for Kenya and Sri Lanka at various times throughout the period.

(iii) Energy and adjustment The low per capita commercial energy consumption and its slow long-term growth rate, coupled with the high energy efficiency of these countries (except for

Peru and Jamaica), indicate that 'adjustment' through sharp reductions in commercial energy use is an unlikely option.

8.9 With respect to economic structure and finance, it was observed that, depending on resource endowment and some other factors, constraints have existed in these (and other) developing countries on the placement of development funds. Bangladesh, Sri Lanka, Kenya, and Senegal have tended to receive funds more easily for agricultural commodity-related projects, while Peru and Jamaica have tended to receive funds for mineral commodity-related projects. No close or causal relationship between the oil crises and inflation rates was found, at least in the cases of Bangladesh, Sri Lanka, Peru, and Jamaica. However, external inflation, both of imported manufactured goods and industrial raw materials, certainly had some effects on short-run budgeting.

8.9.1 The issue of borrowing for adjustment was examined with particular reference to the key IBRD publication on this subject.[1] The propensity to borrow suggested in this publication is not borne out by the actual experiences of the sample countries. The borrowing experience of Jamaica, Peru and, perhaps, Senegal conformed with the projection that oil price increases will automatically trigger extra borrowing, and thus explains the differing rates of increase in borrowing seen at various points of time throughout the study period for at least four of the sample countries.

8.10 As regards the IMF facilities, there was a marked disparity between the demand for such funds and their availability, particularly with respect to the oil facility. This was apparent in the timing of the net disbursements of this and other adjustment facilities in relation to the percentage of export receipts absorbed by the oil account. The data for Sri Lanka (a borrower from the oil facility), Bangladesh, and Jamaica, when compared with IMF facility disbursements, show that the greatest needs for new short-term finance occurred during 1976–8 when the IMF funds were being withdrawn. It is concluded that the IMF facility funds did not, in general, respond to the short-term adjustment needs (i.e. balance of payments problems) of the developing countries as a group because of three major factors: scale (the funds available were never more than 10 per cent of needs); mismatched phasing (the funds were not available in the periods when they were most needed — broadly,

1975–6 to 1977–8); and conditionality. The specific case of Jamaica illustrates the overdeflationary approach of the IMF and IBRD to a short-term problem. Such an approach delays the faster GDP growth, industrialisation, and diversification of the economy necesary to achieve real, sustained adjustment in developing countries.

8.11 In examining the commercial energy intensities of the sample countries it was found that, using the base of barrels oil equivalent of commercial energy used per $US1,000 of GDP in 1979, the countries fell into two distinct categories. The four lowest-income countries, mostly agriculturally oriented, had commercial energy intensities much lower than the average for all industrial countries. Two of these — Bangladesh and Kenya — had commercial energy intensities below that of the Federal Republic of Germany, one of the world's most efficient economies. However, Peru and, in an extreme form, Jamaica were found to be very energy-intensive. For Jamaica in particular this poses direct problems for adjustment in the energy sector. The IBRD in its *World Development Report* of 1981 makes repeated references to commercial energy intensities and adjustment. The figures used by the IBRD lack precision in the calculation bases used, and do not conform with the figures developed by this study. IBRD analysis of commercial energy intensities in developing countries notably fails to attach significance to the very low figures recorded by lower-income developing countries, such as the four in this sample. The IBRD's implicit or explicit price and income elasticity functions for commercial energy demand in developing countries need further examination.

Further, the IBRD's price elasticity models of commercial energy demand in developing countries do not conform with the actual trends for most of the sample countries during the study period. Generally, indigenous commercial energy production, except for Peru, has been concentrated in hydropower (or in natural gas in the case of Bangladesh), and grew consistently throughout the period. On the other hand, commercial energy consumption showed dramatic variability. Except for Jamaica, the countries showed little (very small or zero for Peru, Senegal, Kenya, and Sri Lanka) growth of commercial energy consumption on a per capita basis during 1960–78. Conversely, consumption increases accelerated for most countries (except Jamaica) during 1974–9. This performance indicates that economic trends are more important, overall, than a mere narrow consideration of deficits on oil accounts.

Factors such as the rapid fluctuations in earnings from commodity exports (due to annual price variations) are a major determinant of commercial energy consumption. This behaviour might be termed 'irrational' by certain financial or development institutions because it shows a low price elasticity of demand and a trend towards continuous growth of oil demand. Except for Jamaica, and to a lesser extent Peru, all of the sample countries showed very high marginal GDP growth per marginal unit of commercial energy input.

An analysis of the commercial energy intensities and capital-output ratios for the sample countries (Bangladesh was excluded, primarily because of the lack of a reliable data base) showed a very high positive correlation (0.899) between these two parameters. This strongly reinforces the arguments presented in the preceding paragraph. In addition, the fluid commercial energy demand structure has initiated several problems in the energy sector.

Development in all the sample countries is seen to require more rigid, organised, and differentiated energy systems. In turn, these require higher and more stable levels of commercial energy demand — electrical power system development is a good illustration of the factors involved. The present tendency for 'monopolistic competition' in the distribution of petroleum products in developing countries requires either nationalisation or tighter regulation to ensure greater economic efficiency.

The volume of petroleum imports has affected the adjustment proces of all the sample countries. However, the case of Jamaica seems to be more pronounced than others. Here, about 50 per cent of total oil imports are used exclusively in the aluminia and bauxite industry. It is suggested that the variable terms of trade in conjunction with the high commercial energy intensity of the economy have been at least as important in Jamaican adjustment problems as the single factor of oil prices.

8.12 This study has reviewed the debate concerning the use and significance of non-commercial energy sources in developing countries. In an analysis of the agricultural sector (one of the least commercial energy intensive sectors in developing countries) it is concluded that increased output per worker can only be achieved through increased commercial energy use.

Note

1. IBRD, *An analysis of Adjustment in Oil-Importing Developing Countries* Report 466, Washington DC, IBRD, July 1981.

INDEX